A Prisoner:

RELEASED

by Brian Brookheart

Dedication

*For my loving wife and companion,
Sherry, without whom this project would never
have been completed.*

*And, in loving memory of
my grandmother, Mary Wease,
a precious, godly woman.*

*And, To my dear friend Hib McWilliams.
Hib passed away recently. I knew Hib for 23
years. In that time, I never saw him without a
smile on his face and kindness in his words.
The last day I saw him, he was telling me that
one of his nurses really needed Jesus. He was
concerned about her. That was Hib. He ran
the race, he finished the course, he kept the
faith.*

Hib knew Jesus.

A Prisoner: RELEASED

Copyright © 1997

Fourth Printing 2001

Published by: Brian Brookheart Ministries, Inc.
                     PMB # 509
                     44 Music Square East
                     Nashville, TN 37203

Editor: Sherry Brookheart

Cover Design by: Chuck Strantz

Front Photography: Randy Blain and
                     Illinois Dept. of Corrections
Back Cover By: Double Exposure Photography

ISBN: 0-9661038-0-7

Printed By: Dickinson Press

Table of Contents

PART ONE

CHAPTER
1

PRISON INTRODUCTION

The trip had taken two hours. The course of our drive had been a winding trek through the back roads of southern Illinois. There was a foot of snow on the ground. I had no sunglasses, and the glare had given me a headache—my head was pounding! The two hours I'd spent in the back seat of the car through the winding roads had made me motion sick. As we turned into the main gate, I sat with my head pounding, trying not to throw up. I was miserable.

It seemed fitting that the physical pain I was experiencing accompanied the mental anguish I felt. I was angry, embarrassed and frustrated. Yet, part of me didn't care. It was like a cloud had been hanging over me for my entire life and had pointed me to this moment—this day. Others had told me, "You're gonna be just like your dad." I took that statement as an insult, as well as a prophecy of impending doom. And so, here I was at the young age of eighteen fulfilling their dark prediction.

My mind scanned the events of my youth trying to gain a sense of how I got here, to this place. "Why?" I kept asking myself. This was like a nightmare—and I couldn't wake up! It seemed that every event in my life had funneled me into the prison system.

So. . .here I sat, with hands cuffed and feet shackled, in the back of a sheriff's car. I was on my way to begin serving a three-year prison term.

As we reached the prison, my eyes remained focused on the yellow brick walls, stained from years of coal smoke pouring from the tall stacks. The blizzard had left huge piles of snow at the end of the parking lot. They, too, were stained yellow from the smoke.

The deputy opened the door, and a blast of sub-zero air hit my body. Once again, the physical conditions of the day paralleled the condition of my heart. I was shivering on the outside and stone cold on the inside. With every step toward the gate, my heart grew colder. I was taking it all in, weighing every moment, never to forget this feeling.

The deputy checked his gun at the gate, and we headed toward the receiving center. We walked down a concrete sidewalk through a long corridor with yellow brick pillars. Our steps echoed off the walls.

A convict was shoveling a path through the snow along the corridor. As we passed him, he saw the five books I was carrying and said, "What we got here, a scholar? You know what we do with scholars here, don't ya? We teach 'em how to use a shovel!" I stared at him as we passed on. He laughed as we walked out of sight.

The path brought us through a large steel door into the processing area. A receiving guard signed some paperwork as the deputy handed me over to the prison officials. Then the deputy waved a brief goodbye and left the room.

The processing center consisted of a large room staffed with a mix of about one hundred civilians and convicts. Everyone there was busily working. Civilian workers wore street clothes while convicts wore prison blue. The room was loud with activity. In 1977, computers were rare, so the processing forms were typed in triplicate on manual typewriters. Sounds from those typewriters cut through the murmur of the hundred voices. I sat with a group of new convicts also awaiting processing. It was as if we were invisible. No one spoke to us or even looked at us. We felt like we were nothing.

Finally, a convict with long, thin hair, wire rimmed glasses, and a graying goatee called my name. He motioned, and I followed. The next sequential prison number was placed on a plaque. The number started with 77 because it was 1977, and it ended with 536. It was only January 17, and I was already the 536th prisoner to enter an Illinois prison that year. I never tried to remember the day that all of this happened; it's just that I've never been able to forget.

The number 77536 was written on the plaque. The plaque was then hung around my neck during the mug shot. Although the number is around your neck for only a few seconds, the effects last a lifetime. Once you get that number, you know that you are condemned. Memories fade as one gets older. You forget your best grade school buddy's face, your girlfriend's phone number, or your coach's name. Details of events that seemed unforgettable begin to fade. But you never forget that prison number. It defines who you are.

After the mug shot, I was escorted into another room. I stood next to a long counter. There were ten convicts working. One walked over and told me to take my clothes off. I questioned his order, and he yelled again for me to take my clothes off. So I stripped down to my underwear. The convict told me to take off the underwear. I was standing there in the middle of the room, totally naked and barefoot. All the activities continued around me while I stood naked and humiliated. Another convict motioned for me to follow him. We went into a small shower room. He handed me a bar of soap and a towel that was about the size of a dish rag and then pointed to the showers. As I turned the handle, cold water came out. It was freezing! I finished quickly and dried off as much as I could with the small towel. The other convict walked over to me holding a chemical sprayer, the kind used to apply insecticides to garden plants. He told me to lift my arms. When I did, he gave me two large sprays under each arm. He then pointed the sprayer at my genitals and gave three long sprays. I looked at him, and he said, "It's if'n you got the crabs." Still naked, I walked back into the larger area. The convicts asked what size I wore and then handed me some clothes. I've always wondered why they bothered asking my size. The orange jump suit they gave me was twice my size and six inches too short. I was given a very lightweight jacket, three pairs of boxer shorts and some white socks.

A guard led me to a receiving dorm. There I was assigned a blanket, sheet, pillow and bunk. The guard walked me over to the door, put the large brass key in the lock, and opened the door to the dorm. As I walked in, every head turned to see me. Convicts watched as I walked over to a bunk, began to make my bed and organize my locker. Within thirty seconds they surrounded me. Some were sharing information about regulations and what to expect from the guards. One guy showed me how to make a bed—prison style. Others asked questions and made small talk. One convict asked me for the bottle of mouthwash that I was issued at receiving. The mouthwash was 25 percent alcohol—he was going to drink it. That particular brand of mouthwash tasted like lighter fluid. Knowing I would never gargle with it, I handed the bottle over to the guy, and he seemed thrilled.

I lay on my bunk until early evening. About sundown a guard yelled that it was time for everyone in the dorm to go to the mess hall for dinner. The inmates started toward the front of the dorm, so I grabbed my light jacket and followed the crowd.

It was the coldest January in Illinois history. That

week the temperatures had fallen to 26 degrees below zero. All of the convicts in the dorm filed outside and down the concrete corridors. Sub-zero wind blew through my oversized jumpsuit, and in a few seconds I was shivering cold and my teeth were chattering. I had no gloves, no hat and only one thin pair of socks. The mess hall was about two blocks from the dorm. I was counting the seconds until we could get to the building. My feet got so cold, so fast, that within a few seconds each step became painful. Finally, the line stopped as we reached the building. I thought the ordeal was over, but the door never opened, and we just stood there. After a few minutes passed, I heard the two guards talking about their problem. My dorm was not scheduled for the mess hall for thirty more minutes. The guards discussed whether to take us back to the dorm or make us stand outside in the bitter cold. After a few minutes, they decided to make us stand outside. The two guards went inside and watched us through the window. For thirty minutes we stood there—grown men freezing in dangerously low temperatures, and none of us could do anything about it. We stood there like cattle for thirty minutes. When the time finally came, the mucus in my nose was frozen solid. The guards were laughing as they opened the door to let us in.

As we entered the mess hall, the line split into two. We all walked to either side of the large room. Each of the 750 seats was filled, and it was extremely loud. Convicts were screaming at each other and at the new cons in orange jumpsuits. This was my first look at the general prison population.

Above the seating area was a group of guards manning machine guns. The machine guns were the prescribed method of regaining control if a riot or fight broke out. If a convict decides to kill a guard, there is no other solution. The numbers are simple: there are 750 convicts against ten guards. Most people believe that prison guards carry firearms. They do not. The guards are at the mercy of the convicts. The machine guns could not save a guard's life, but if the machine guns opened fire, they could easily kill everyone in the mess hall. They are there simply to remind the convicts of the consequences of any aggression.

I followed the line, grabbed a tray and was issued my first, unforgettable serving of prison food. It was horrible. Bus stations have bad food. The Army, convenience stores, most hotels, truck stops and mall restaurants also have bad food. But no food on the planet compares to prison food. It is the most unsavory, tasteless concoction known to mankind.

Convicts with discipline problems are usually assigned to work in the kitchen. Therefore, the worst convicts cook the food. No one in prison would even mention it if they found roaches, mice, mouse droppings or any other objects in their food. Imagine eating at a hamburger stand staffed by murderers, thieves, rapists, and other mentally disturbed men. If sickening objects didn't accidentally fall into the food, they were most likely put there on purpose. On this particular evening, we ate the delicacy that I aptly named "gristle-burgers." A "gristle-burger" is a hamburger filled with crunchy bits that cannot be chewed. Closer examination showed that they had ground up the meat, bones and all, and served it to us.

After the meal, we walked back through the cold to the dorm. The thermostat in the dorm was set at 60 degrees. With sub-zero temperatures outside, it was much colder than 60 degrees inside. To keep the heater running, we placed a wet towel over the thermostat, but even then it was still unbearably cold. When the lights went out, I lay shivering.

I couldn't sleep. After only a few hours, a whistle blew. There were loud voices outside. I didn't know what was happening, but I knew that something was wrong. The noise continued throughout the night. In the morning we were told that a convict had gone over the wall in an escape attempt. The prison was located in a river bottom, so the convict had hidden there to avoid the authorities. When the guards tracked him down three hours later he was wearing the lightweight prison-issue jacket and leather shoes. He had caught his glove on the razor wire at the top of the fence in his attempt to flee. His fingers and toes were frostbitten by the sub-zero temperatures, and they were eventually amputated. He could have frozen to death and was fortunate to have survived. When I left prison, the glove was still hanging there; the guards never took it down. It was a quiet reminder of the failed escape attempt. It was haunting to consider that a man could become so desperate that he would attempt an escape during such weather. I had been in prison less than twenty-four hours and yet it already seemed like forever. What would a month feel like? A year? Would the pressures become so great that I'd be willing to risk my life for a chance at freedom? These questions flooded my mind.

The next day began with a trip to the mess hall. I can't remember what was served during this adventure in prison cuisine. It was something like "pineapple upside down sausage gravy." The rest of the day was spent being processed. For part of my processing I was taken to a room with about two hundred school desks to undergo a psychological evaluation. The evaluation consisted of six hundred questions; all questions were to be answered with a "yes" or a "no." Some more amusing questions were: I like to play kick-the-can; I like manly-looking women; and, I am a secret agent of God. I don't know much about psychological testing, but I bet that everyone who took that test was pronounced "insane." Well, at least I felt crazy after the test!

For the next stop we walked about three blocks through the concrete corridors to a large, yellow brick building. I waited for about an hour, and then a panel of three men interviewed me. They asked repeatedly if I had any tattoos, scars or needle marks. My answer was no. They didn't believe me.

At lunch time, we marched back to the mess hall for a serving of "tree bark casserole." Dessert was "frog pudding." It was delicious. I was really putting on the pounds. During that afternoon I had my first chance to go to "the yard." Every prison movie has the classic "yard" scene. You've seen it. There are always musclebound body builders with big tattoos pumping iron, guys who could have made the NBA slamming basketballs, small gangs of toughs standing around protecting their turf as if they owned part of the prison, and lots of guys looking for someone to bum a cigarette from. This wasn't a movie; I was seeing the yard in real life. And yes, in real life what I saw were musclebound body builders with big tattoos pumping iron, guys who could have made the NBA slamming basketballs, small gangs of toughs standing around protecting their turf as if they owned part of the prison, and lots of guys looking for someone to bum a cigarette from. I had two hours to kill in the yard. In my usual satirical approach to life, I marched my 145-pound body over to the weight area and began pumping iron. My career as a body builder lasted about thirty minutes. I enjoyed it for a short time, but I quit because the weights were so heavy.

I had been in jail for two weeks before being transferred to prison. In jail, you just sit around all day. There is no way to exercise. So the prison yard was a welcomed event. After weight lifting I ran some laps and played basketball. The level of talent displayed by the convicts in all the sports was impressive. Playing basketball was fun, but tempers flared a few times during the game. I found that rule number one is: You never forget where you are and who you are with—that you're surrounded by the outcasts of society in prison. These outcasts are prone to settle disputes with their fists. Generally, most of the problems were minor, and the games were fun.

Late in the afternoon, I got word that I was

scheduled to see the job assignment committee. This committee consisted of two men sitting at a metal table. When I sat down they didn't look at me. They talked about me, but not to me. It was as if I wasn't there. They glanced down at their notes and spoke among themselves. A convict had told me earlier that the kitchen was the worst place to work. Hepatitis or syphilis were the only two things that would keep a convict out of the kitchen. Within twenty seconds the job assignment committee had assigned me to the kitchen. As I was leaving, one of the men asked me if I had any diseases. "Only syphilis and hepatitis," I replied. "He's had both of them," the guy said. "You're going to the laundry," the other yelled. "Thanks," I said, as I exited quickly. I felt like I had dodged a bullet.

I returned to the dorm just in time to get back to the mess hall for dinner. Again, an unbelievable meal! On this particular evening we enjoyed a dish that I called "snow tire souffle." They can make delicious food out of a used tire. Most states throw used tires away, but not in this prison. These convicts really knew how to cook a tire.

It had been a rigorous day filled with activity, most of which consisted of waiting. I began to realize how tiring it is to wait. However, waiting is a normal part of being in prison. During "waiting" times there was absolutely nothing to do. At the doctor's office there are always lots of magazines to chose from. During rush hour the radio helps to pass the time. In prison no one cares about you. There are no radios, no magazines, and no televisions. You are left alone with just your thoughts.

Either that, or to talk with the other convicts. The time passes very slowly. In prison, all you think about is time: how much time are you doing, how much time has passed, and so on.

After dinner I lay on my bunk for some rest. The guy next to me was sobbing out loud. He was about forty-five years old, bald on top, and he had a little round belly. At first the noise didn't bother me because I thought that he'd quit soon, but it continued all evening. Finally I couldn't stand it any longer. I asked him what was wrong. He looked up at me. Tears were running down his face as he cried out, "I could have had a house full of kids if I hadn't been a drinking man." With that, he buried his head in his pillow and cried the rest of the night.

Actually, what alcohol had done to this guy, drugs had done to me. The circumstances weren't similar, but the result was the same. His life was destroyed, and he was a broken man. He was crying real tears as he examined his life. Although I recognized his despair, I couldn't offer him any help. I was in the same prison he was in.

The next morning as I was making my bed a convict walked up to me. "You don't know this yet," he said, " but you're going to the commissary today. That's where you buy stuff, like a store. You brought money in with you, so I got a list of stuff you're gonna buy me. Get me two packs of smokes, get me some stamps, 'cause I gotta write my ole' lady. Get me some cookies, the kind with the chocolate stripes on them. Bring all this stuff back to me. Here, take this list. You got it?"

"I got it," I said as the guy turned around and started to walk away. This was a moment that I had been waiting for. It's common knowledge that in prison you have to stand your ground when confronted for the first time. If you don't fight, you are sentenced to a subservient existence. Once you have been pushed around, you'll always be pushed around. These convicts aren't nice and sweet. They have concern for no one. The prison society is one that preys on the weak. So you have to prove that you are not weak. This was the first time someone tried to push me around. I was going to fight. I didn't feel like taking orders from some idiot convict. As the convict turned to walk away, I wadded the notebook paper into a ball and threw it at him. It hit him right in the back of the head. He spun around fast with an attitude like he was going to kick my butt. He stared at me for a minute, snorted with disinterest, then walked away. I knew that at six feet tall and 145 pounds, I was not the most imposing figure, and I couldn't fight at all. What he saw when he stared at me was a stone-cold, crazy kid. My hair looked like the lion's from the Wizard of Oz. It was frizzed out down to the middle of my back, I had a goatee, and there was a fire in my eyes. Nothing mattered to me. I didn't care if I lived or died. Going to prison didn't upset me. Furthermore, there were eighteen years of frustration and hatred inside me, brewing in my heart. I was not about to be held captive by some loser inside the prison. Dying was a better option, and he saw it in my face. He turned and walked away, and it was a wise decision for him. Had he tried anything with me, I would have killed him. I would have waited, picked my moment and killed him. I was that angry, frustrated and bitter. Beyond that, I was suicidal.

A few days earlier I had begged the deputy who drove me to the prison to shoot me. I had it all planned. We could make it look like an escape. He declined my offer. I honestly didn't care if I lived or died. The bully convict had seen that in my eyes and went on to an easier mark.

A few hours later I was lying on my bed reading a book when I heard a loud commotion. Two convicts were fighting. Everyone in the dorm ran over to see the show. They were fighting right in front of my bunk. I dropped my book down a few inches so that I could see over the top. One fighter had the other by the shirt and pants and was bashing his head into my bunk. His face was being cut up by the steel frame. The crowd cheered for each blow.

By the time the guards got to them, blood was streaming from the loser's face. He looked like he'd been in a car wreck. During the fight I didn't move an inch. I showed no interest or involvement in the scrimmage. The fight happened within two feet of my bed; the loser was smashed into my bed; yet I was a million miles away from the fight. It was not my problem. It came and went without me. I was not involved. As the guards removed the convicts, I realized that I had learned a valuable lesson about prison. I needed to fight my battles and my battles only. I stayed within myself mentally and emotionally. The fight came and went, yet I was not involved.

As a new convict, I was trying to get a grip on prison by talking to the other convicts. I soon learned that convicts are world-class liars. Prisoners sit around and lie to each other for hours. One convict told me that he was a general contractor. I asked him which buildings he built. He told me that he built skyscrapers. His most prized project was the world's tallest building, the Sears Tower that soars above the Chicago skyline. Other convicts were "doctors", "lawyers", and "bankers". These were people who knew that we knew that they were lying, yet no one ever challenged their lies.

Those who admitted to being criminals on the street often exaggerated the size of their crimes. An armed robber might brag about the large amounts of cash he'd always had on the streets. One fifty-year-old man was bragging about the fact that he had written $28,000.00 in bad checks. I asked him how much time he received for the crime, and his answer was seven years. I told him that came out to $4000.00 a year, and that he could have made more money working any menial part-time job at minimum wage. He looked me dead in the eye and said, "I wrote $28,000.00 in bad checks." With that I decided that I would not waste my time trying to converse with other inmates.

Prison is a society devoid of true friendship. Two convicts would become "friends" and share information about each other, as friends do. Repeatedly I would see that same information used by one convict against another. When this happened, the result was usually a fist fight or a stabbing. No one in prison can be trusted.

It is a vicious society in which everyone is trying to take advantage of everyone else. I realized that within hours of arriving, and I immediately began preparing myself for total solitude.

In doing so, I began to think about my life—not just sitting around replaying the "glory" years, but really examining the events in my life. I thought about different decisions that had led me to prison. At age eighteen, society had decided that I needed to be separated. Was I really that bad? If this was my life at eighteen, then what did twenty-five hold for me? What about thirty? Would I spend the rest of my life in prison, being told what to do by guards? What would I do with my life? Everyone that I knew on the streets would answer these questions in the most negative way. No one gave me one chance in a million to make something of my life, and who could blame them? My performance so far hadn't been too great. My life had been a struggle, and I had failed. How did I get here? What led me to these depths at only age eighteen?

CHAPTER

2

THE EARLY YEARS

Home was a little shack on the south side of a small southern Illinois town. My mother, brother, sister and I all lived in four rooms. There was a front room, a bedroom, a kitchen, and a bathroom. Linoleum was laid over wood planks on the floors. Ugly wall paper covered the thin walls. With the slightest bump on any one of the walls, a hole would be created. So, holes scarred every wall in the house.

Heat was provided by a wood-burning stove that sat in the front room. We did not have a bathtub or shower, and there was no hot water. There was no telephone, no television, no garage, nothing. Winters were unbearably cold. My mom never remembered to get wood for the stove; we'd either run out of wood, or she'd order the wood late. And worse yet, when we did have wood it was usually green, and it wouldn't burn. The result was bitter cold every winter.

One year my brother, sister, and I were all sick. My mom went to the neighbor's and called the doctor, and he came to our house to see us. When he walked in, I remember that he yelled at my mom for it being freezing in the house. "No wonder these kids are sick," he screamed. Mom made no excuse. The doctor went outside, got some wood, built a fire, and left.

Wind whistled through the cracks in the house. There was a constant draft strong enough that it would blow out a candle. Wind wasn't the only thing that came through the cracks in the walls. Roaches, mice and rats came through them as well. The house was infested with roaches and overrun with mice and rats. At age five, my favorite pastime was killing mice. I'd sit on the counter in the kitchen, and when mice ran across the floor, I'd throw our can opener at them in an attempt to impale them. I also trapped them when I could get a trap. There were so many mice in our house that a trap would catch one within just a minute or two anytime that I'd set it, any time of day. Countless times I awoke in the night to mice running across me and across my bed.

In spite of all of that, my early years were somewhat carefree. I played outside in the ditch and entertained myself while my brother and sister were in school. It wasn't bad at all. It was later in these early years that two things happened to change my perception of life.

The first thing was that at age six I started school. Until I started school, I had no peers with which to compare my life. At school, I was forced to compare my life with theirs. My life was devoid of all the things that others considered necessities. We had no television, telephone, car, or other common items. On cold or rainy days, their parents drove them to school. I walked. Their clothes were clean and pressed. My clothes were old, soiled, and wrinkled. Their shoes fit well and were new. My shoes were worn until the soles had holes in them. Often throughout my school years I was forced to wear my shoes until the soles were completely worn out and my feet touched the ground when I walked.

About halfway through the first grade-school year, my shoes were completely worn out. I absolutely couldn't wear them anymore. My mom didn't have the money to buy new shoes. The only thing that I had to wear was a pair of house slippers. The slippers didn't look like shoes. They were yellow with fur around the top that formed a lion's head. I hated to wear them, but I had nothing else to wear. I walked into school wearing the house slippers. To this day, I remember that feeling of horror as my peers saw the slippers. They teased me without mercy. As a first grader, I couldn't cope with the intense pain of that day. The incident was just another reminder that I wasn't equal with the other students.

The second thing that changed my perception was the topic of my father. It didn't take long for my peers to realize that my father was not living with me. It was only natural for them to ask where he was. I did everything that I could do to hide the truth from them. The truth was that he was serving hard time in a federal prison, and I had never met him. My only picture of him was what I had pieced together in my mind through family stories. It was difficult to answer their questions, so I never did. I avoided them when I could and lied when I couldn't. My home town was small, population 5,300. Many people knew my dad's story. So, about halfway through the school year, a student came to school with information about my dad. Somehow, he had found out the true story. Before lunch time, he had informed every one of my classmates about my dad.

I knew that now my peers saw me through the knowledge that my dad was a criminal. With that information now public knowledge, my attitude began to harden. Now I was damaged goods—an outcast—and I felt like giving up. My only defense was to act tough and to withdraw.

I loved the part of school that involved studying and learning, but I hated the social aspect. Whenever a social situation involved conflict, my peers could always use the subject of my dad to even the score. I heard it continually. My first grade year marked the first time anyone told me that I was going to turn out just like my dad. Those words cut deep from the first time I heard them, and I grew to hate them more and more each time they were uttered. It was a curse that would be spoken over me a thousand times throughout my life.

I lived a deprived life, and even the most innocent social events highlighted that fact. In first grade we had "show and tell." My classmates brought in things such as Indian artifacts from Oklahoma, or souvenirs from Cape Kennedy, or a new snorkel fire truck that sprayed water—a grand variety of interesting items. Every week I would sweat over what to bring. My mom had an eighth grade education. We lived on the welfare system. I had a brother, a sister, and a shack for a house. We fought each day for enough food to push back hunger pains. Neat items worthy of being shown off at school were a million miles away from my immediate life. So every week I would agonize as I got up with nothing to show. I'd struggle as I declared, again, that I had forgotten that today was show and tell day. It seems to me now that the teacher could have made this practice voluntary so that the less fortunate kids, like myself, wouldn't have been embarrassed. The practice continued throughout my first grade year.

The first school year was almost over, and it was springtime. One day my class was getting ready to go down the hall for music class. Neither the music class nor the music teacher had ever been my favorites. I told the boy sitting next to me that I hated the class. I was telling the truth. Unfortunately, my regular teacher overheard my remarks. When the class was over, she asked me to stay. As I sat there, she told me that she had heard what I had said. She began to pull my hair, twist my ears and slap me in the face. This was happening from a teacher that I really liked. The abuse continued for an entire hour. I was in shock, and there was nothing I could do. At the end of the hour, she marched me down the hall and made me apologize to the music teacher. The event caught me completely off guard. The teacher gritted her teeth as she slapped me. That was the day that I realized she hated me. She really hated me. And I hated her back, as well as the school, my peers and my life.

By the end of my first year in school I knew that I was different from the other students. I had learned that I was inferior. Through it all I had learned to hate the world as a whole and my peers individually. I discovered that there was nothing that I could do to win the favor of the teachers. They knew my family background even before I walked into the class. Their negative perception of me was set before they ever saw my face. They let me know very plainly that I was not equal, and I got the message loud and clear.

When summer vacation came I was thrilled to get back to my home routine of playing in the ditch and killing rats. Throughout the summer I pondered the events of the preceding year. My longing to go to school had been shattered by the realities of my life.

My brother Ed and I spent the summer terrorizing the neighborhood. Every night we victimized a different house. One night we pulled the lever on an outside fuse box and turned off all of the electricity to a house. The neighbors came out of the house, flashlight in hand, stumbling around until they got to the switch and turned it back on. We'd hide in a ditch, rolling with laughter as we watched them. Then we'd wait until they were back in the house for about ten minutes, and we'd pull the switch again. Of course, they eventually called the police. But, what were the police going to do? They couldn't catch us, and they didn't scare us. They couldn't stake out the house for the entire evening. We kept the pranks up for the duration of the summer. This was the cheapest, best entertainment we had. Though we never broke or stole anything, we did irritate many people! Once we broke into a house during the day. There was a bag of malted milk balls sitting on the table and a picture of John F. Kennedy hanging on the wall. When the owners arrived home, we were inside the house throwing malted milk balls at the picture of John F. Kennedy. The owners of the house became irate. The lady started crying because it was shortly after the assassination in Dallas. We were threatened with punishment over this act, but nothing ever happened to us. And so, the daily entertainment continued. Consequently, I always had trouble writing the annual "How I Spent My Summer Vacation" paper that teachers always require during the first week of school.

During the third grade, our teacher had a routine of reading a book to the class for about twenty minutes immediately after lunch. One day when I walked into class, the teacher grabbed me and wrestled me to the floor in front of her desk. My toes and nose were touching the floor as I lay flat on my stomach. "You stay there until I tell you to get up," she commanded. She walked to the front of her desk, sat and started reading. Obviously, no one was looking at her. Every eye in the classroom was focused on the spectacle that she had made of me. I stayed there on the floor until the twenty minutes had passed. Why was she treating me this way? I did not understand why I was being punished. Other students in my class got into trouble occasionally, but I was the only person who received punishment like this that degraded instead of instructed. The twenty minutes finally passed, and I was permitted to return to my seat. I felt embarrassed, ashamed and worthless. I later heard that one of my classmates had told the teacher that I had misbehaved during lunch time. Without questioning the accusation, she found me guilty, and that humiliation had been her sentence. She never treated other students like that. I knew that this wrath was reserved for "special" students. Sometimes teachers, and people in general, fail to understand the gravity of their actions; but those twenty minutes of meanness that others soon forgot cut like a knife into my heart. The humiliation troubled me for years. As a teenager I often thought of killing that teacher. She should have realized that little boys grow up. Events like that one caused me to gradually grow cold, hard and calloused.

During the fourth grade, our principal was planning to retire. A retirement ceremony had been planned in which a student from each class (first through sixth grade) would present the principal with a retirement gift. Our teacher decided that a dozen roses would be the gift from our class. The teacher wrote "ROSES" on one slip of paper and put it in a box along with many blank slips. She told the class that we would pass the box around the room, and whoever drew the slip that said "ROSES" would be allowed to make the presentation to the principal during the ceremony. The box came to me, and I drew a slip of paper. When I unfolded it, the word "ROSES" was there. I immediately began to think of flattering things that I could say to the principal. When the box had reached the last student, the teacher asked for the "lucky student" to raise his or her hand. I cheerfully raised my hand into the air. When the teacher saw my hand, she said, "We're going to have to do this one more time." So the slips were collected, another student drew the word "ROSES," and that time, it was good enough. I stared in disbelief as I realized what had happened. The teacher offered no explanation; the contest had been won fairly, but I was denied the opportunity. Clearly the teacher did not want me to represent her class during the retirement ceremony. This "singling out" repeated itself often in those years, and was a daily reminder that I wasn't equal with the other students. Being put down, picked on, and teased were common occurrences. I remembered every putdown, every joke and every bit of laughter directed at me. My heart grew cold, and I became a ticking time bomb ready to explode.

During the first three years of school, my peers and teachers were my biggest enemies. However, during the fourth grade, a new enemy came to call. For some reason, my mom's welfare checks would no longer buy enough food to last through the month until the next check came. We would have food for two or three weeks and then it would run out and we'd go hungry. It was even worse during the winter, when my mom had to buy wood for the stove.

During those weeks without food, I'd go to school with my stomach burning from hunger. It was the worst feeling I'd ever felt. I would run home after school each day to see if Mom had found some food during the day. The despair was overwhelming when night after night the answer was "no." I'd go to bed hungry, hoping that tomorrow would bring food as a relief. A week without food seems like an eternity to a child. It's like a cancer that eats up your existence. You think of nothing except getting rid of the hunger. I was a hard, proud little guy, and I never would have asked for help from anyone. However, my sister began to go around our neighborhood to beg for pocket change. Sometimes she'd get enough to buy us lunch at the school cafeteria. Those meals were the best I'd ever tasted. The first time I ate at the cafeteria, I was amazed that the other students left the foods they didn't like. Hominy is a good example. No one would eat it. But I ate it. The fact that I didn't like the flavor and texture was irrelevant. I ate it because it would push back hunger for a few more hours.

My aunt lived five miles outside our little town. On Saturdays, instead of sitting around starving, my brother and I would walk to my aunt's house. She had a goat farm on twenty acres, and her husband had a minimum wage job as a night guard in a local factory. He was also a drunk. They were poor by anyone else's standard, but to us they were rich because they usually had food. So, we'd walk to the farm regardless of the weather. When we got there, we'd tell her that if she'd let us eat first, we'd work the rest of the day. It was hard work, but it felt like heaven compared to hunger.

Like other children in their formative years, I should have been playing games and having fun. I should have been developing a positive attitude toward the world. Instead, I was burdened with the cares of life.

Imagine being nine and having to fend for necessities such as clothes and food. Because of this, I never remember having a childlike view of life. I was always somber and serious minded.

My summers were spent working on my aunt's farm. Her husband, Tom, was the closest thing that I had to a father figure. Tom had several brothers. All the brothers had wives and kids. On weekends, they'd come to visit. They all drove old junk cars, and every one of them drank too much. When they got together, the beer flowed. They sat around all day and drank while I mowed the lawn. I never complained; I was the only one getting paid. When they were ready to leave, their cars would never start. There they were, grown men without shirts or shoes, standing around a car, leaning into the hood, trying to talk through slurred drunken speech. How clearly I remember beer bellies, profanity, and bad tattoos. That was life for me on the farm.

During the school year, the teachers were not concerned with my situation. It was obvious to me that they did not care. I would sit there in class, starving, and they'd criticize me for lack of concentration. They did nothing to win my trust. I never shared the secret of my existence with them, or anyone.

At home we were always out of food. One day I went outside to play with my dog, Penny. I called her and she didn't come to me. She wouldn't respond to a tug on her chain. When I knelt down in front of her doghouse, it was obvious that she was dead. My dog Penny had starved to death. Even as a fourth grader, I understood the gravity of the situation. I was heartbroken and didn't have another dog for over twenty years.

One foodless stretch lasted for weeks. The hunger was unbearable; I looked everywhere for something to eat. The only thing in the house that was edible was a large jar of liver extract pills and a five-pound bag of sugar. I hid the two items. Every time I'd start to hurt from hunger, I'd eat a handful of liver extract pills and spoonfuls of raw sugar. I still don't know what a liver extract pill does or what it contains, but they filled my stomach and caused the pain to stop—that was good enough for me.

The mice and roaches that infested our house were as hungry as we were. Anytime food was brought into the house, they tried to eat it as fast as we did. Countless times we'd find roaches in our food. We got to the point where it didn't matter that there were dead roaches in our food. We brushed the bugs aside and ate it anyway. The same applied for food infested with mice. Nothing stops you from eating food when you're hungry. Roaches, mice, or mold—they made no difference. If you're hungry, you eat it.

During my fourth grade year, Mom called Ed and me in for a talk. We sat together on the couch. She had a very serious expression on her face, and we wondered what was wrong. She explained that my dad had been released from prison. He had been paroled to his mother's farm. It was an hour drive from our house. The big news was that Dad wanted to see us. I hadn't really thought about the reality of the day of his release. I was curious. What kind of person was he?

About a week later, my brother and I boarded a bus for the hour ride to meet Dad. I will never forget the feeling of stepping off the bus knowing that I was going to meet my dad. We walked down the steps of the bus and stepped onto the ground. A man walked over, said he was our dad, gripped our hands and we started to walk away. The introduction was so quick that I hadn't gotten a good look at him. As we walked, I tried to look up and clearly see his face.

The weekend was uneventful. I had no real feelings of love, hate, joy or sadness relating to my dad. He was a man that I didn't know. We returned home Sunday.

After a few months, Dad was hired by a pest control company. He sprayed houses to get rid of bugs. He drove his company car over to pick up Ed and me. Since he was now in the pest control business, he asked us if our house had bugs. We said that it did, so Dad took it upon himself to spray the house. As he began to spray the insecticides, roaches began to run all over the floor. The floor and walls were covered with the pests. As he continued to spray, more roaches came out. When he was finished spraying, there were so many roaches on the floor that we swept them up with a broom.

My dad, Ed and I got in the car and began the hour drive back to his house. As we pulled away from the house, Dad began to yell at us about the sickening conditions in which we lived. He kept asking how we could live in such filth, and didn't we know better? I remember thinking that if he had been there for us as a father, maybe we wouldn't live like that. However, it never occurred to him that he had abandoned us and that we were surviving in the best way we could. The scolding lasted for the duration of drive.

As the months passed, my dad asked us to live with him. Eventually, we were persuaded that living with Dad was a good idea. My brother went first. He wrote letters in which he described eating at malt shops that served triple thick malts and great cheeseburgers. It sounded like heaven to me, so within two months, I, too, moved in with Dad.

The only good thing about living with Dad was that there was always food. Hunger was eliminated from my life. However, during that time my dad met a woman and married. Together they treated us like dirt. I have often wondered why he wanted us to live with them. He spent months trying to convince us to move in. Because he put forth so much effort, I thought that he really cared for us. He didn't. He and his wife were abusive and angry. I never grew to liked them.

Dad often told people that I was his favorite son. That statement sickened me. I didn't even want to be his son, let alone his *favorite* son. Life with him drove me crazy. My dad piddled. By that I mean that he piddled with trivial matters. He was always working on a mechanical project. For instance, an article in Popular Mechanics would interest him. He'd spend days talking about building an electric car or something like that. At first I believed him, but I soon learned that he wasn't really going to do any of the things he talked about. He was a dreamer, and he never put any actions behind his thoughts. This was not the man that I had hoped my dad would be. He also had personality traits which he blamed on prison. For example, he would begin to yell uncontrollably when someone locked the front door. Locks "freaked him out." The list went on and on. I began to think that he used the prison experience as a way to get attention. The list of things that bothered him grew and grew. We were always wondering what would "freak him out" next.

One day we were outside working on his Volkswagen van. He told me to go around to the shed and get him a ball-peen hammer. I didn't want to tell him that I didn't know what a ball peen hammer was. That sort of thing could send him into a rage. So, I ran around to see if I could find something that looked like a ball peen hammer. The minutes seemed like hours as I searched frantically for the tool. Finally, I gave up and told him that I could not find the hammer. I knew that this would bring on a fit, and it did. He yelled that I was stupid—any boy should be able to identify a ball-peen hammer. What was wrong with me? Why was I so worthless? He was right. Most boys could have found the hammer. But, most boys aren't raised by a woman with an eighth grade education while their dad is in prison. He criticized me for my shortcomings—shortcomings which were due to his neglect and the lack of a father's influence in my life.

Soon after I moved in with him, Dad took a job working the night shift in a factory. It was heaven for us because he slept during the day, and we seldom saw him. One day after school a friend of mine and I were playing in the backyard, rolling big barrels around and having a great time. Suddenly, I looked up to see my dad storming out of the house carrying a big stick in his hand. He grabbed me and began to beat me. My friend ran home to safety, but I was left alone with this furious man. I could barely breathe through the pain. Eventually, I lost control of my bodily functions, and wet and soiled my pants. The beating continued for some time, until finally he stopped. "Don't ever wake me up again," he commanded as he stormed back into the house. I lay on the ground, a pitiful mess, gasping for breath and stinging with pain. After a while, I regained my composure enough to go inside and clean myself up.

That evening I sat in my room and thought about the beating. This was the last thing that I wanted my dad to be. My hope had been that my dad would bring normality to my life. My hopes and desires were the same as any kid's. I dreamed about Dad taking me to a baseball game or pitching a ball with me in the yard. In my dreams he'd walk with one arm around my shoulder, pulling me close and telling me that he loved me. My dad had come home, and I wanted him to be a knight in shining armor who would save me from my plight. Instead, all he had to offer was mental and physical abuse. The same dad who'd brought shame on my childhood was now savagely beating me. I remembered this beating years later, at age twenty, when I was working the night shift in a factory. Little neighborhood girls were playing next door. Their laughter woke me up. My mind flashed back to the day

I woke up my dad. "So that's why he beat me," I thought. For a moment I pitied him, and then I rolled over and went back to sleep.

My father's abuse continued to increase. He began to make my brother and me wash all the dishes. That in itself was not abuse; but, if my father found a dirty dish or spoon, he would make Ed and me wash every dish in the house. He would make us wash every glass, cup, pot, pan, and piece of silverware in the entire house. If he found a dirty dish at midnight, he would get us out of bed and force us to wash dishes all night long. It didn't matter that we had school the next day—we washed all night anyway. Often we'd drag into school exhausted after being up all night. It was a terrible time for us.

Dad named these dish washing nights "G.I. parties." He threatened us with them. When the "G.I. parties" had become commonplace, Dad reverted to more physical forms of violence. There was no telling what would set him off. One day he "caught me" on the back porch. He had a belt in his hand. He beat my legs with the belt until they bled. To this day, I don't know what I did to deserve that beating.

At one point in my youth, I began taking guitar lessons after school. After a few months, I was still struggling to play songs, as it takes years to become proficient enough to sight read and play music. However, my dad was undaunted by this fact. On one particular evening he brought in gospel sheet music and told me to play a song. Ed and Dad's wife were there, and they were to sing along. I looked the music over and told Dad that I couldn't play the song; it was too difficult. He told me to play it. I tried to play it, and he screamed that my playing didn't sound like the song sounded on the album. I was playing the best I could. Dad, his wife and Ed sang along. I was sitting on the sofa, with my guitar on my lap. My shins were exposed. When I'd make a mistake, Dad would kick me in the shins with his heavy leather wingtip shoes. He kicked me hard. My shins were hurting, and I was supposed to concentrate on the sheet music. At every mistake, he'd take a step back and kick me. My legs were black and blue from the abuse. I soon lost interest in playing the guitar. He actually acted like he was doing me a favor by kicking me; he said it was "motivation."

Abuse from Dad continued until the summer following the sixth grade. Ed was going into his sophomore year. He'd played football during his freshman year; he was always fighting at school—and he was turning into one tough guy. One day we decided that enough was enough. We were tired of Dad's abuse, and while Dad could whip one of us, he couldn't whip both of us. We told Dad that we wanted to talk to him outside. He was irritated, but he agreed. Ed and I each got a baseball bat and went outside with the bats over our shoulders. At the first sign of aggression from him, we were going to unleash years of hostility.

He came out of the house. We explained to him that he had abused us and that we were tired of it. It wasn't going to happen again. If he thought that it was going to continue, he could speak now, and we'd present an opposing point of view. Our point would be reinforced, of course, with the baseball bats. We were primed, ready, and full of adrenaline. Dad must have known that we were growing up and that we were dead serious. He negotiated with us, and the abuse stopped.

In spite of Dad's new found kindness, I couldn't take living with him anymore. I packed up my belongings and moved back to Mom's house. I was entering the seventh grade and I was growing rapidly. The first thing I noticed when I got to Mom's was that I was bigger than she was. For the first time in my life I was totally in control. My mom was uninvolved in my life. She didn't even try to guide me.

One instance that reflected my reluctant independence was that at this point in my physical development, my teeth came in crooked. I desperately needed braces. Mom was on welfare, so we had a public aid medical card. One dentist in the area was licensed by the State of Illinois to put braces on kids. His office was a one-hour drive from our house. I knew if I could only get to his office, I could get braces and my teeth would be straight. Mom didn't have a car, so I asked relatives and friends for a ride. None of my family or friends would take me to the dentist. No one cared enough to sacrifice a few hours to improve my appearance for a lifetime. As a child, no one has to tell you that you're worthless. With enough putdowns you figure it out on your own. I never got a ride to the dentist, and I never got braces.

Entering the seventh grade, I had an attitude, and I was convinced that I was cool. Teachers, school and discipline were boring. I was a first-class menace. My grades were terrible because I never studied. I did only what I had to do to get by.

During the evenings, I'd hang out on the streets downtown. Sometimes I'd mill through the trash dumpsters in the alleys. Drunks would come out of the taverns, and I'd talk to them. At first they were funny. Later I learned that they weren't funny, just drunk. My whole life revolved around killing time. I was just waiting, on hold with no purpose to my existence. No one cared enough to help me, and I had no idea where I was going. One evening I ran into a group of older teens. They told me they were going to burglarize a store downtown and asked if I wanted to help. It sounded exciting to me, so I went along. We climbed up to a second story window, pushed the window in, and entered the building. I was the guy inside the store grabbing merchandise off the shelves and bringing it to the back of the store. From there the other boys took it out of the store. We were almost done with the burglary when I looked up and saw a night security officer outside rattling the front door. I panicked, but somehow he didn't see me. He turned and walked away into the night. After this close call, I was ready to end the burglary. We climbed down out of the building and made our getaway. For my efforts, the guys gave me a little transistor radio that didn't work.

After the burglary, I hung around those boys almost every night. They were much older than I was, so I tried to act tough. Our evenings were spent doing low level mischief around the town. One night I stole a ten-speed bicycle from the front yard of an upscale neighborhood. I was about two blocks from the house when the chain came off the bike. While I frantically tried to put the chain on, a police car pulled up. The cop asked me if I was having trouble. My heart was pounding. I told him that the chain had come off my bike. He was so polite. He shined the spotlight on the bike so I could see to make the repair. I finally got it back on. As I rode off, I thanked him. When he was out of sight, I took the bike back to where I had taken it from and walked home.

One day, the superintendent of schools called me into his office. My older friends had spray-painted obscene graffiti on the walls of a school, and he assumed that I had been with them. I denied being there, and he let me go. Whenever a crime was committed, I was already on the list of usual suspects to contact—and I was only in the seventh grade!

I began to stay away from home at night. If I couldn't find a friend who'd let me stay over, there were always abandoned cars that would serve the purpose. If I couldn't find anything else, I'd sleep in a barn. Anything was better than going home.

At this point in my life, I was headed for serious trouble. I didn't care about anything. It would have continued to get worse had it not been for a girl at school who took an interest in me. She took me home to meet her mother. Her mom and I also became friends, and she welcomed me into her home every night. With that invitation, I had a family structure. I had a television to watch and records to play—it was wonderful. Best of all, my friend's mom fed me every night. When she'd go to the store, she'd ask me what I wanted to eat. At the end of the night, she'd drive me home. Her name was Betty, and she was the nicest, kindest person I'd ever met. I love her to this day. With that stability in my life, I started to play basketball for the seventh grade team. We had a good year, and it was really fun.

One night I heard a loud noise in the front yard of my house. I looked out to see my dad throwing sacks out of his car onto the ground. After about fifteen minutes, my brother Ed came into the house. Dad had decided to start abusing Ed again. Unfortunately, by now Ed was a street-hardened mean-machine. He was not going to take any more abuse from Dad, or anyone else. Dad had tried to push Ed around one more time, and Ed hadn't gone for it. He and Dad got into a fight, and Ed "cleaned his clock." He broke Dad's dentures and scarred his face. My dad's wife jumped in to help Dad, so Ed broke a bottle of syrup over her head. Dad loaded Ed and his clothes in the car and brought him home.

It was great to have Ed back. He hadn't, however developed any "normal" social skills. He would do or say anything to anyone. That aspect of his personality assured the fact that life with him would never be boring.

CHAPTER

3

HIGH SCHOOL

August is a hot and humid month in Illinois. The weather is miserable. It's not uncommon for the temperature to be 90 degrees and the relative humidity to be 90 percent. As school started, the heat made it unbearable to sit in class. That was all the excuse I needed to skip the first few weeks of school.

When I returned to school, I was immediately taken to the principal's office. Truancy was sufficient grounds to send me to a boy's home. As soon as I left my meeting with the principal, I called Dad. Within a week I moved.

Moving in with Dad depressed me. To release the depression I felt, I started writing poetry. One of my first poems started like this:

What in the hell am I living for
and why in the hell do I suffer more
than anyone whoever walked this earth
I've been sad ever since my birth.

That poem summarized my life to that point. It is a sad commentary for a high school freshman to write such things.

By the time I moved back in with Dad, he had become a preacher. Are you shocked? I was. He admitted to me that it was nothing more than a job. The hours were good, and he didn't have to punch a time clock. Moving in with him meant that I had to play the role of "the preacher's kid." I never did get the hang of it. Suddenly, I was supposed to know church etiquette. I wasn't too good at pretending. One day I was painting at Dad's church. To make the time go faster, I played a tape through the church sound system. That wouldn't have been all that bad, except the tape I played was "Steppenwolf—Live." Some elders came in while the song "The Pusher" was playing. That song has very graphic lyrics and much profanity. Dad was reprimanded. Privately he'd tell me that he didn't care what I did, he just wanted me to keep it under control so he wouldn't have to take the heat for my actions. He knew that I wasn't into the church scene, and he didn't care.

By springtime Dad found a new church, and we moved to Pennsylvania. Within days of our move to Pennsylvania, Dad and I were at war with each other. Finally, he drove me to the bus station in Pittsburgh and sent me to live with Mom. Conditions at Mom's house were terrible, so I contacted a friend in northern Illinois. His family offered to let me live with them while I finished out the school year. After the school year, they drove me back to southern Illinois.

Altogether I made five different moves during that first year of high school. I was an antisocial, withdrawn loner, and I never learned to make friends. All of my life

I had been told that I wasn't as good as others. I saw myself as totally and completely inferior.

During that summer I went to a party. As I walked in, someone handed me a beer. Later in the evening, a guy sitting next to me lit some marijuana and passed it around. I was already drunk and had no inhibitions, so I smoked the marijuana. By the end of the summer, I had graduated to hard drugs, and my appetite for them was insatiable.

When my sophomore year of high school started, I was in no frame of mind to be in school. I didn't care about any of the subjects. Because of the five moves during my freshman year, I was already behind in my classes.

One day after school I came home to find that my mother was missing. After searching the house, I found a note. In the note, Mom said that she had moved to another town and was going to marry some man named Harry. She left forty dollars and wished me well.

That evening Ed and I went to her new house to ask her to come home. Her boyfriend met us at the door, pointed a pistol at us and told us to leave and never come back. The pistol was enough to convince me that we really weren't welcome.

For the rest of my sophomore year my only interest was surviving. My time was spent between the homes of my relatives. I never stayed anywhere long enough to wear out my welcome. The school year finally ended, and somehow, I passed all of my classes.

During the summer I went to work at a bicycle

factory. The factory required workers to be at least age eighteen, but I was only sixteen. Somehow, the personnel director never asked for proof of my age. I guess years of struggling through life had aged me.

During that time, my days started at 11:00 p.m. Previously, I had never been inside a factory. As I walked in, I was overwhelmed by the noise and the smell. It was loud, and it smelled like burnt motor oil. I had never worked an eight-hour work day, and the first night seemed like eternity. I ran a large metal press that formed bicycle handle bars. It was boring. The boredom made me sleepy. Staying awake was a struggle, but within a couple of weeks I got used to the routine, and it wasn't so bad. There were a lot of guys at the factory who supplemented their income by selling drugs, and so to stay awake, I took amphetamines.

I was sixteen years old and making money. For the first time, I had a steady paycheck. I bought a van and fixed it up a little. With every paycheck I bought clothes and shoes—plenty of shoes. I spent the rest of my paycheck on drugs. I did everything that I could get my hands on. Within ten minutes of waking up, I'd smoke marijuana. Throughout the day I'd take LSD, mescaline, heroin, and cocaine. The most dangerous habit that I had was taking thorazine tablets while drinking whiskey. It was inexpensive, so I could afford to do it every day. The combination of drugs and alcohol turned me into a zombie. I was like a sleepwalker. My eyes were open, but I couldn't think.

As the summer ended, I faced another school year

of living on my own. I knew that working at the factory and going to school would be too difficult to swing, but I didn't want to quit school. I didn't know what to do. With all of that weighing on me, I packed up my clothes and a quarter pound of marijuana, boarded a bus and went to live with Dad.

When school started in Pennsylvania, I walked in wearing the new clothes that I had bought during the summer. It was then that it occurred to me that no one knew me there. No one knew that I was underprivileged and from the wrong side of the tracks. People treated me differently than they had in my hometown. I could make friends easily and life was really fun. The marijuana that I brought with me ran out, and I didn't bother to buy more. I was really enjoying myself without it.

About a month after school started, I ran for Student Senate and was elected. I applied for a job at a high-end furniture store and was hired. When basketball season started, I tried out for the team. The coach was really great. He was young, energetic, and a stickler for discipline. He earned our respect. For the first time in my life, everything was going well. I had made some close friends. My job was going well. My boss trusted me enough to let me drive his Lincoln Town Car. They were teaching me the business, and I was eager to learn. The Student Senate gave me a leadership opportunity at school. It was a great time in my life.

My Christmas holiday began on that same wonderful note. I spent time with my friends and we had basketball practices together to get ready for a tournament. Then, one day while I was walking home from practice, I looked up toward my house to see a U-Haul trailer parked at the front door. I ran up the hill and asked my dad what was going on. He said that we were moving to St. Louis so that he could go back to Bible college. I was shocked and saddened. My life had been so happy in Pennsylvania, and now, with no warning we were moving. Dad gave me two hours to tell my friends goodbye. He told me to hurry because we were leaving that night.

Within a few hours we were on the road heading for St. Louis. As we traveled down the road, I started to really hate my dad. I realized that he hadn't considered me at all in this move. He had no concern for me, and therefore I decided to have no concern for him. Moss had never grown underneath my dad's feet. He was a rambler—just one step above a drifter. He stayed in one place just long enough to encounter some trouble, and then, at the first sign of conflict he was gone. It was the classic "fight or flight" syndrome—when conflict arises a person either stands his ground and fights, or retreats from his troubles and runs. My dad ran, and he's been on the run his entire life. This was just another move for him, but he was taking me from the happiest situation I'd ever been in.

Another thing that hurt me about the move was that Dad had conned some good people into financing both the move and his return to college. The couple he had swindled were in their mid-seventies. After retiring from the Army, the husband had started a successful business. His wife made custom draperies for high profile customers. They weren't rich, but they were set for life. Unfortunately, they had fallen under Dad's spell. It was a difficult position for me to be in. I knew that he was conning them, but I couldn't tell them. They wouldn't have believed me. They were bright people, but they never saw through him. Once my Dad wanted to go to a pastor's convention held at the Stouffer Hotel in Washington, DC, so he called the couple. He managed to talk suggestively about the convention. It took a few minutes, but Dad convinced them to pay for the trip. I don't how much money he took them for, but the hotel was first class. Not only did he get the money, but we drove one of their new Cadillacs to Washington, D.C.

Now, he was driving a rented truck across the nation with a pocket full of their money. I'm sure that he had convinced them that he'd go back to college, get his degree, and then do some grand work for the Lord. But I knew that Dad just wanted to hit the road again. The easiest way to get on the road was to con those nice people out of their money. I know they never got their money back.

When we got to the Bible college, Dad and his wife moved into married housing. My residence was a 12' x 12' room at the men's dorm. From January until May, I seldom saw Dad. When we were together, we fought. Finally the semester ended, and I graduated from high school. I moved back to my hometown.

There I met a woman through a mutual friend. One night she told me that she was sad and depressed.

Apparently she had devised a scheme to defraud an insurance company by burning her house down and she was sad that the plan had fallen apart. By the end of the evening I agreed to burn her house down for her.

I made several gasoline bombs, and at about midnight I set my bombs around the house. One bomb was thrown through the window. I'd seen this done a hundred times on television. It was supposed to break and slowly start to burn. Instead, it exploded and blew the window back out at me. I quickly threw the other bombs into the house and drove off. The house burned to the foundation.

As I drove away, it was like I was living inside of a mental fog. I felt no emotion about the crime that I had just committed. I had no thought of being caught, and I felt no remorse. After the crime, I simply went home to bed. The next day I saw the owner of the house. She was glad that I had done the deed.

About a month passed, and no one had connected me with the fire. However, my friend started to worry. She was scared. She went to the police and confessed. She gave the police her statement which said that I had committed the act of arson. Within a few days, the police arrested me. At age seventeen I was arrested and convicted of a Class X felony.

Because I was still a minor, the sentence was two years of probation and a $500.00 fine. Before I graduated from high school, I was a convicted felon.

In spite of this, I decided that I wanted to attend college. A government rehabilitation organization for troubled youth offered to help pay my tuition. Before they could help, though, they needed a psychological profile. They sent me to see a clinical psychologist. The doctor gave me an eight hour battery of tests. At the end of the tests, she told me that drugs had damaged my mind and impaired my thought processes too much; I was incapable of academically performing at the college level. She further predicted that my life would consist of menial dead-end jobs. Based upon her tests, the government agency refused to waste their money on me. So, I decided to try college on my own.

CHAPTER

4

PARTY ON

As I entered college I gradually drifted back into the old habit of using drugs. Being in school gave me the opportunity to hang out with an older group of friends. A daily search for drugs was the center of our lives. It was our goal to find stronger and stronger drugs. It was all that we talked about: availability, quantity, quality and price. We developed a network of connections so that we could get various items. We went to different dealers for different drugs. Usually our "connections" were in other states. One of our best, but most dangerous connections was in Detroit. Each time we networked with a dealer, we came home with a new load of chemicals. Upon our arrival home, the word would soon spread, and within an hour there would be thirty or more drug addicts in a room shooting up our new supply. I was looking for a reliable supply for marijuana when a man approached me at a party to asked if we could do some business. We negotiated a deal to have five pounds of marijuana delivered to my house every Saturday. I had known the man for years, but I never asked him to do business with me. When we were moving enough stuff and were considered trustworthy, he approached me.

I could not believe my eyes when the pot was delivered the first time. I had envisioned a sophisticated technique for delivering the product.

That dream vanished when a ten year old Chevy pulled into my driveway. The driver staggered to my door carrying a beat-up grocery sack filled with pot.

Another of our connections had a laboratory where he manufactured PCP. We bought it directly from the lab, so the stuff was uncut and dangerous. I warned everyone to be careful and to take less than the usual amount. A few hours after delivering the PCP, I returned to the house. There were people lying everywhere. Most had fallen out of chairs or off of beds. No one was moving. I thought they were all dead. When I tried to revive them, I found that they were alive but unconscious. They had ignored my words of caution and had overdosed. Everyone became sick, but they all lived. A lot of the drugs that we sold were "pharmaceutical," made by major drug companies. We typically bought cases of pharmaceutical amphetamines. We bought them with the seal still on the bottle, one hundred bottles in a case, with the plastic wrap still over the cases. They came straight from the manufacturing plant. They were the exact pills that doctors give to those who request "diet pills."

Taking large doses of amphetamines is rough on the body, but at least the stuff was made under controlled circumstances. Street drugs are dangerous because you never know where the chemicals are made. There's no way to tell what's in them, how strong they are, or what was used to "cut" them. The only way to find out if they are "good" or not is to take them. That is one reason why junkies die of overdoses when some unusually pure cocaine or heroin comes into their city.

For most of my freshman year, I made regular drug runs. I'd go to Detroit, pick up a load, and party. With the profits I bought a better van, but I blew the rest of the money.

Everything seemed to be going well. It was springtime, and I was about to finish my freshman year of college. My 18th birthday was coming up, and I asked my friend Kim if she'd accompany me. She agreed. We went out and had a blast. It was the perfect eighteenth birthday, spent with my best buddy.

I spent the next day drinking whiskey and listening to music with Ed and a friend, Marty. Kim had wanted to date Marty, so during the day, I told him about Kim. Kim came over at about 7:00 in the evening, and she and Marty hit it off right away. Then we all went to a party; there were at least a hundred people there. I saw some old friends and spent most of the evening with them. About midnight we decided to go to a restaurant. I asked Kim if she wanted to go. She declined and agreed to meet me at my house later. She thanked me for setting her up with Marty. I headed for the restaurant.

I got back to my house some time later, but Kim never showed up so I went to bed. In the morning, I awoke to someone coming up the stairs. I glanced over expecting to see Kim, but it was my friend "Griz." He walked over and sat on my bed. His head was hanging down, and he sighed, "What a night." I asked how the party ended. He looked at me and said, "Oh no! You don't know about the wreck, do you?"

"What wreck?" I asked.

He blurted, "Marty's dead, and Ted's in critical condition. They were in a car wreck."

"Whose car were they in?" I asked.

"Kim's," he mumbled. "She's in critical condition at Good Samaritan."

Within five minutes I was dressed, in my van and on my way to see Kim in the hospital. The drive was 90 miles. I drove as fast as I could. During the drive I thought about what I'd say to her.

When I got to the hospital, I went to the nurses' station to ask for directions to Kim's room. The attending nurse looked confused, and pointed to the head nurse. I repeated my question to her. She, too, looked confused and asked, "Are you family?"

I lied, "Yes, I'm her cousin."

"Wasn't the family notified?" the nurse questioned.

"What do you mean, 'notified'?" I asked.

Then she looked me straight in the eye and said, "She expired during the night."

I was grief-stricken. Kim was my closest friend. We were always together. I loved her. She was a person who understood me well. She had died, and now I was dying inside.

Kim had earned a full college scholarship as a musician. When a new song played on the radio, she could listen to it and then play it perfectly. But her life ended because she was drunk. That night at the party she drank too much. Marty and Ted helped her to her car because she could barely walk. She only had one major road to cross on her way home. When she got to that road, she pulled out in front of a semi-truck. The collision killed Kim and the two friends who helped her to her car.

Kim's funeral was a clash of two cultures. Her mom attended a Baptist church, so half of the crowd consisted of little church ladies and Baptist ministers. The other half were Kim's friends. We were a band of musicians, drug dealers, high school dropouts, alcoholics, and drug addicts. Before the funeral, her mother told us to be on our best behavior. Five of the pallbearers were from the Baptist church. They were straight, well-groomed guys. Then there was me. I looked like someone from a freak show. The pallbearers and minister rode in the hearse. As we pulled away from the church, they made it clear that they blamed me for Kim's death. I had nothing to say in my defense. I felt responsible, and I was emotionally crushed. My mind was tormented by the questions, "Why did I take her to the party, and why did I leave without her?" One day I was celebrating my birthday with Kim, and the next day she was dead. The guilt was overwhelming.

After the funeral, all of our friends came to my house for a party. We partook in the usual assortment of drugs, this time "in Kim's honor."

One night a girl came to my house and announced that she had decided to start taking drugs. She brought a list of things she wanted to try. I asked her if she really wanted to do this, and she answered with a defiant yes. I filled her "prescription" and gave her instructions on what to take and how much. She left my house.

A few hours later, I called her house to check on her. Her mother answered the phone, and I asked to speak with Linda. Her mother screamed that she was violently ill and that she couldn't come to the phone. I hung up. Linda had taken all of the drugs on the way home and had overdosed.

Undaunted by the first experience, Linda started taking drugs daily. I'd see her occasionally at parties. She wrote me letters, but I never answered. She was another lost and lonely soul, crying out for help. No one heard her, and no one cared.

One day after school she loaded a handgun, took it into her bedroom, put it in her mouth, pulled the trigger, and blew her head off. She was only seventeen.

The list of my friends who died in their youth is long: Carl was electrocuted. Ron, Brax, Marty, Mark, Ted, and Kim died in car wrecks. Phil, the county drug hotline director, shot up too much heroin and died of an overdose. Madonna was hit by a car. Randy, Linda, Brent and Whitey shot themselves. John hung himself. Teresa died giving birth after her husband had beaten her. Five years later her husband died in a car wreck. You get the idea. It seemed that our mortality rate was as high as in a war zone.

By this time I lived in a two-bedroom house in a middle-class neighborhood. There were people partying at my house twenty-four hours a day, seven days a week. We were a constant menace to the neighborhood. For example my buddies might decide to get on a motorcycle at 2:00 in the morning and dig up the neighbor's yard by revving the engine and popping the clutch. Cars were coming and going at all hours of the night. There were doors slamming, music blasting, people yelling, and horns honking all night long. There were always at least four people sitting in the kitchen playing cards. It seemed like one card game could last for six months.

Throughout the months I lived in that house, not one neighbor ever complained about the noise. The only explanation that I can offer is that they were afraid of us. At one point I didn't pay my rent for six months. Again, the landlord never even came over to see what was going on.

During the summer, our supply of drugs was running low. My connection in Detroit had new products, and we needed drugs for a big Fourth of July party. I drove up and bought the drugs at a nice house in the Detroit suburbs. It was the '70s and times were different. Rival dealers weren't killing each other for drug turf. You could do deals with thousands of dollars in cash and not worry about being killed. We didn't carry firearms; we never needed them. In fact, it was a social time. But within a decade, dealing drugs would turn violent. Gangs and gangsters would control the drug trade and be willing to kill each other for control of drug turf. But back then, we were relaxed because we trusted each other.

One night I was coming home from a party with a friend when I noticed red lights flashing behind me. I pulled over, and an Illinois state policeman walked to the side door, opened it, and began searching my van.

He didn't talk to me; he just kept searching. Soon another police car pulled up. Now, three men were tearing my van apart. A small quantity of marijuana and a concealed weapon were found. My friend and I were arrested, searched, and then placed in a police car.

Once the car began rolling toward the jail, we removed bottles of PCP and cocaine that we had hidden down our pants. We lifted up the bottom cushion of the back seat and stuffed the goods through the cracks.

Inside the jail, the state policeman started the interrogation. He asked me repeatedly where I got the marijuana that they had found. I never answered, but he kept asking. The years of abuse had made me hard and cold. My exterior was calm, cool, and collected, and I had absolutely no respect for the police. I hated cops, and there was no way that I was going to answer their questions.

After two hours of questioning, the jailer put us into a cell. As soon as the door locked behind us, my friend started to panic. He was scared. He insisted that he couldn't live with the knowledge that the cops would eventually find the drugs that we'd placed in the car. I told him that as soon as someone else was seated in the car, they could not prove that the drugs were ours. But nothing would ease his fears. He insisted that we had to get the drugs out of the police car. We argued about it until we went to sleep. In the morning when we bonded out of jail, we agreed to meet in a few hours to discuss a plan of action.

I went to a restaurant for breakfast. While I was

eating a guy I barely knew walked up to me and said, "Man, I heard about that stuff you put in that cop car. I hope you get it out." My heart sank. My friend had panicked and told some people, who told other people. Within an hour, the word had spread like wildfire. With that many people knowing the "secret," I knew that we were finished.

After breakfast I met with a group of my close friends to discuss the problem. We smoked some pot, did some cocaine, and drank beer. Then we discussed how to get the drugs out of the cop car. Eventually we stopped talking about removing the drugs from the car, and someone suggested that we alleviate the problem by blowing up the cop car. Soon the plan was set: explosives would be placed under the car to blow it up. This would incinerate the drugs in the car. Someone mentioned that the explosion might kill the cop and his family. Our overall response to that was, "So?" Plans were completed, and the meeting adjourned. Somehow, our entire plan seemed plausible. Our rationale was typical of anyone with a mind blinded by drugs. Any sober person could have seen that this plan was insane on many levels. Yet it seemed totally reasonable to us at the time.

Can you see how easily a life is destroyed by drug abuse? I was arrested because of drugs; yet I got stoned before the meeting just a day later. I didn't know it then, but I was making the biggest decision of my life, and I was making it while I was stoned.

With our thought processes impaired, we planned to commit a burglary to steal the explosives we needed to carry out our plan. We were certain that the second crime of blowing up the car would cover the first crime of burglary.

That night my friend and I were in my van when four police cars followed us. Their lights lit up the night. Their sirens were screaming. Before I could get out, the cops rushed the van, dragged us out and threw us on the ground. I asked what they were doing. "Shut up if you wanna live," one of the deputies yelled. "Ladies, are you comfortable, ladies?" they asked.

I cursed them, and they roughed us up even more. The exchange of profanity continued and so did the beating. Finally, they put us in separate police cars. Once inside the deputy laughed at me and told me that they had found the drugs we'd placed inside the cop car. I, of course, "didn't know what he was talking about."

As we drove, I continued to swear at the cop. Inside the jail, I was fingerprinted and charged with four felonies related to the drugs we'd placed in the cop car and one for attempting to blow up the cop car.

At the arraignment the next morning, my bond was set at $50,000.00. At the hearing I pleaded "not guilty" to all charges. The most serious charge they had against me was "delivery of cocaine," which carries a sentence of one year to life. When the judge said "life," I started to laugh uncontrollably. I thought that with the way my life had gone, I'd surely get a sentence of "life."

Life! If my sentence was life in prison, I didn't want to live. On the way back to the jail, I asked the deputy to shoot me. I begged him, but he declined. Back at the jail, the deputy told the jailers that I asked him to shoot me. The jailers put me on a suicide watch. For a month I looked for a way to kill myself, but I couldn't find a way.

Being in jail was so boring that I counted the concrete blocks in my cell. I must have counted them a hundred times. One's entire existence in jail is experienced inside of the mind. You talk to yourself, you think about the past, and you dream about the future. To make it worse, I went on a hunger strike. The guards would give me food, and I'd throw it at them. They hated me because I caused trouble. They retaliated. They'd leave my light on all night so that I couldn't sleep. They'd wake me up if they saw me sleeping. I'd hit them with a bowl of corn flakes in the morning, and the cycle would repeat itself.

Each day a deputy came into my cell to ask for the names of other drug dealers. I knew if I didn't cooperate with him soon I would be going to prison for sure. If I did give names, they'd "go easy on me." But, every day this speech brought the same response from me. I had no desire to give the names of other dealers to the police. This was the '70s, and I was from the "old school." You don't save your life by destroying someone else's. I knew the consequences of my actions—that prison was a possibility. For a threat to be effective, the person being threatened has to fear the threat. Prison did not frighten me, so I refused to talk.

While I was in jail, the police never got a warrant to search my house. They never realized that if I had drugs in my van, I might also have them at my house. I

59

am so thankful for that. If they had searched my house, I'd still be in prison today.

After forty days in jail, I finally made bail. A pharmacist friend in Detroit heard that I was in jail and sent the money. I was released to await my court date. As I got into my van in the parking lot of the jail, I noticed a bit of marijuana lying on the floor. While I was still in the parking lot of the jail, I lit it up, and I smoked it all the way home. When I got to my house, I found it totally empty. All of my possessions had been stolen. My "friends," knowing that I was in jail, came over and helped themselves to my stuff. I couldn't believe that they would do this to me. Again, this was the '70s and we all spoke about peace, love and brotherhood. The brotherhood ended when they knew they could rob my house and get away with it. They even stole my clothes.

I cleaned my house of drugs for the six months that I was free, and I still found drugs when I finished. The cleaning was just for safety's sake. My main goal during my time away from jail was still to stay heavily under the influence of drugs. I took everything that I could get.

Trying to survive was a struggle. I had no money and no plans. My life revolved around killing time until my court appearances. My house was virtually empty. All of the utilities had been turned off. I had no electricity, so I lit the house with candles.

The state's attorney had offered my partner a deal if he would testify against me. If he testified that the drugs were all mine, he'd get a reduced charge with jail time.

He was considering their offer, so I threatened to kill him. During a face to face meeting, I asked him which side of his head he wanted blown off. I was really angry, but I was no killer. He did not know it, but the real menace was our Detroit connection. These people were a real danger to him. They had heard about our arrest, and twice they came to Illinois to question me. I knew that if they ever even thought that we were going to turn them in, they would have killed us both. I reassured them that my partner was going to testify against me, not them, but they still wanted to kill him.

I finally persuaded them that I could take the heat and do the time. They eventually believed me when I told them that they would never be mentioned. Consequently, no one was killed. My partner never knew how close he came to dying.

The deal that they offered him was no surprise to me. His parents owned a business in town. They were well-respected citizens. Beyond that, the lawyer they hired was the states attorney's law partner in his private practice. I knew that I would be convicted and that I was going to prison. My only goals were to postpone it for as long as I could and to get as little time as possible.

Because of my firsthand experience, I believe that the judicial system in America is basically a game. All it takes to play the game is money. While in the system, you can't see the truth for the game. Sometimes attorneys don't want the truth. They are just playing the game. In my case, I thought that the police didn't have 'probable cause' to search my van, so we spent months at hearings trying to suppress the evidence. We exhausted all of the legal arguments, without success. The police were a part of the game. They were trying to win, and sometimes even they bent the rules.

Unfortunately, the game kept me from truthfully examining myself. I was consumed with the fact that the cops and state's attorney were not playing the game fairly. I never took the time to admit that I was guilty—that I had committed every crime I was accused of and many more! Often, those who win at the judicial game lose at life. They "get off" and therefore never confront the real problems of their lives. In fact "winning" in court can harden people even more. They are never forced to stop and truly evaluate their lives. By winning, they lose.

Finally, I arrived at the place where all my attempts to avoid prison had failed. One of my best friends in the world was going to testify against me. Without his testimony they would have never been able to prove that the drugs discovered in the police car were mine. With his testimony, I knew that I would never win in court. Things did not appear to be in my favor. Furthermore, it was election year and the D.A. wanted to get a cocaine conviction under his belt because it would help his chances for re-election. He would have done anything to convict me.

My attorney managed to negotiate a one to three year sentence in exchange for my guilty plea. For a court appointed attorney, that wasn't a bad deal. If I'd had money for a private attorney, rather than a "public defender", perhaps I could have really played the game. That's the judicial system. For the most part, "justice" is for sale in America. Those who have the money to get a good attorney almost always get out of jail. If the state's attorney has to work hard on your case, your odds of being convicted are greatly reduced. They typically go after the easiest convictions. As a wealthy person, if you are convicted, you are more likely to receive a suspended sentence or probation. I suppose that is why I never met a wealthy man in prison.

Examples of this are everywhere in our society. A friend of mine was once busted with 65 pounds of marijuana. But he was from a rich family so not only did he never see the inside of a prison, he never saw the inside of a jail. The officers who arrested him knew who he was, so they let him sit in the sheriff's office until his parents could come down and bail him out.

But life is not a game! What a man sows, he will also reap. Those who "win" at the judicial game don't necessarily win at life.

It had been six months since I was bonded out of jail. To escape the pressure that I felt, I sank into the abyss of the heaviest drug use of my life. I went on a binge. I took LSD, mescaline, peyote, and barbiturates like mandrax, quaaludes, thorazine, valium, and nembutal. To get up, I took amphetamines or uppers like preludes, fastins and black beauties. I also took heroin and cocaine and smoked pot. I drank excessive amounts of alcohol. During this binge I overdosed three times. Once I thought I was going blind. When I came down my vision was blurred. The second time, I lay on my sofa for a week unable to move from the effects of PCP. The third time my heart began beating uncontrollably. I thought it was going to explode. Nothing I tried would slow it down. I couldn't go to the hospital because the police would be notified, so I rode it out. My heart pounded for hours. My blood pressure had to have been "off the chart." I'll never know how my heart survived the stress of too much cocaine and speed.

After six months of playing the judicial game, I couldn't postpone the inevitable any longer. The state's attorney had me, and he knew it. All of the drug, weapons, and conspiracy charges had been filed while I was still on probation for arson. It was a forgone conclusion that I was going to prison.

I pled guilty to one count of possession of cocaine under the negotiated plea. The judge sentenced me to one to three years in an Illinois prison. I remember that during the proceedings I couldn't concentrate. I had taken drugs all morning. Even the knowledge that I would soon be sent to prison for possessing drugs did not make me stop using them. After the proceedings, a friend drove me to jail. I wasn't nervous. Prison was inevitable and I just wanted to get on with it.

At the jail I was fingerprinted and then given a solitary confinement cell. While waiting to be sent to prison, a severe blizzard dumped fifteen inches of snow in our region of Illinois. That kept me in jail for two weeks. Finally, the weather cleared and I was on my way to prison.

CHAPTER

5

THERE IS HOPE

One night, while I was lying in my prison bunk thinking about my life, I began to consider how all of the predictions made about me had come true. I *was* in prison just like my dad. That fact killed me inside. I was tormented by the tragedies of my life, and I was embarrassed by my actions.

After about one week in prison, the effects of the drugs upon my mind began to fade. I was sober. With my thoughts and actions no longer clouded by drugs, I realized I didn't want my life to end in ruin. Some convicts spend their entire lives serving one prison term after another. That was one option for me. It was a strong possibility that I'd become institutionalized and spend my life behind bars. I saw examples of this daily: One convict had served his three-year sentence. Finally, he was approved by the parole board for release. Before his release, he was given a three-day furlough so that he could go home and get his affairs in order. During that three-day furlough, he was arrested for burglary. He was caught trying to drag a safe out of a gas station. That convict had learned nothing during his three-year stay in prison. What if I had turned out like him?

As the hours dragged on, the torment of my life weighed heavier and heavier upon me. I felt like I was going crazy. All I wanted was some relief from the terror in my mind.

One night I began to call out to God. I wasn't the best at praying, but I asked God to help me. As a child growing up in poverty, we didn't have a television. I remember that my favorite entertainment was reading a Picture Bible. It was written like a comic book, but the stories were clear. Those stories came back to me, and I cried out to the God that I had read about as a child. With utmost sincerity I asked God to forgive me of my sins and to help me. All that I knew to do was to ask Him to heal my life, and I began doing that every night.

My plans weren't grandiose—all I wanted was help in the simplest form. So I laid in bed and prayed at night, partially because it was the only way that I could find relief from the torment in my mind. Every night before I went to sleep, I had to pray. I asked Jesus for help. After a while, I found enough peace so that I could sleep.

One night in particular, I began to hear a voice stir inside me saying, "Brian, there is hope for you." Over and over again I heard, "Brian, there is hope for you." That night I cried out to Jesus like I never had before. In my life, no one had ever offered me hope—no one. The psychiatrist said that my mind was destroyed by drugs. The judicial system said that I was beyond hope and locked me up. My family had abandoned me. My friends had turned on me and robbed my house. I was completely alone. But at my lowest hour, Jesus was sticking with me, encouraging me. He was whispering to my heart, "Brian, there is hope for you. Brian, there is hope for you."

That night a breakthrough came. I gave my life to Jesus. He became my Savior and Lord. He washed away my sins, and I knew it . Nothing had changed on the outside, but inside I was born again. In the midst of the worst circumstances, hope had been placed into my heart. In the Bible, the Holy Spirit is called the Great Comforter, and I found Him to be just that (John 15:26).

Jesus had become my Savior inside the prison walls. Skeptics refer to this phenomenon as "jail house religion." This derogatory term refers to prisoners faking Christianity to gain an easier prison stay. What a fallacy of epic proportion! Professing Jesus inside a prison is no way to become popular. When the average person accepts Jesus, he will more than likely tell his family and coworkers about his experience. The extent of his risk is a little verbal persecution; perhaps he'll be ridiculed by disinterested friends. A prisoner lives with the men in his cell block twenty-four hours a day, seven days a week. If they become irritated, the result could be much worse than mere ridicule. It could be deadly.

The apostle Paul wrote about his desire to share the knowledge of Jesus Christ with all men in Romans 1:16. "For I am not ashamed of the gospel of Christ: for it is the power of God unto salvation to every one that believeth; to the Jew first, and also to the Greek." Paul said that he was a debtor. In other words, he was unworthy of the mercy of Jesus. In my life, I was the worst of the worst; yet, somehow Jesus had mercy upon me. Who was I? No one! Yet God's great grace was given to me! Paul was a debtor, and so am I.

When we accept Jesus, we owe everything to Him.

In order to be obedient to Him, I owed it to those around me to tell them the Good News, that Jesus gives hope! How could I be ashamed of Jesus? There I was, a prisoner, yet He took me as His own. He was not ashamed of me, so there was no way that I could be ashamed of Him. Jesus was the best that I had ever had, and I shared Him with others. When we share Jesus with others, we release the power of God unto salvation (Romans 1:16).

Something real had happened in my heart. This was not "jail house religion." I had really met Jesus Christ. My sins had been forgiven, and I was free from bondage. I was delivered from that torment in my mind, and I wasn't going to keep that victory to myself. My prison ministry started the day I accepted Jesus. In my heart He was the King of kings and the Lord of lords, so I preached Jesus to mass murderers, rapists, thieves, drug dealers, to those who would listen and to those who would not! Some received the words with gladness; others became angry and threatened me. But no one ever harmed me physically. God protected me because I feared Him more than any man. I relentlessly shared Him with others as I felt Him lead me.

One day while I was at work in the laundry area, I began telling one of my coworkers about Jesus. It was obvious that he was getting mad, but I kept talking. My fellow worker was blinded to the Gospel, just like the apostle Paul predicted he would be. My words about Christ enraged him so much that he put his nose about a half an inch from mine and threatened to kill me if I kept talking. I told him I just didn't want him to go to hell. After that he backed off and went back to work.

As Christians, we know that what we are sharing is the greatest gift in the universe. Yet sometimes people reject what we share with them. Why is that? When the light of the Gospel beams down upon their lives, it exposes their sin and their inherent need. That exposure makes people uncomfortable and often times angry. I call it "defending their misery." People who don't know Jesus will argue in support of the very sins that have made their lives miserable. For example, before I submitted to Jesus as my Savior, I would have argued in favor of drugs, even though drugs, drug abuse and fellow drug users were precisely what had ruined my life. II Corinthians 4:4,5 states,

In whom the god of this world hath blinded the minds of them which believe not, lest the light of the glorious gospel of Christ, who is the image of God, should shine unto them. For we preach not ourselves, but Christ Jesus the Lord; and ourselves your servants for Jesus' sake.

Matthew 10:27,28 says, *What I tell you in darkness, that speak ye in light: and what ye hear in the ear, that preach ye upon the housetops. And fear not them which kill the body, but are not able to kill the soul: but rather fear him which is able to destroy both soul and body in hell.*

After giving our lives to Christ, our only fear should be the fear of the Lord, a respect and awe for Him, and the desire to do His will. We cannot hold back from others the life that He has given us.

Matthew 10:32,33 tells us, W*hosoever therefore shall confess me before men, him will I confess also before my Father which is in heaven. But whosoever shall deny me before men, him will I also deny before my Father which is in heaven.*

After a while, prisoners began coming to me when they received bad news from home; they'd come to me for prayer. Once a prisoner named "Gums" (He had no teeth!) got a letter from his wife telling him that his little girl had been diagnosed with leukemia. Gums and I prayed for her. A few weeks later Gums received the wonderful news that his daughter had no sign of leukemia. God had answered our prayers from prison!

The prison world is filled with darkness: the darkness of sin, the darkness of hopelessness, the darkness of despair, and the darkness of a life without God. As a Christian I discovered that I was called to be a light shining in that darkness. While in prison I wrote a simple poem about light:

Light

Sun shining in the morning
your colors are aglow
Son of God who lives in me
Lord, you know I love you so.

Sun shining oh so bright
bringing life unto the morn

Holy One who made that sun
It's of your Spirit that I'm born.

I think about the way light is
You know it always conquers night
and all the darkness in the universe
can't put out one little light.

So brothers and sisters I tell you now
we are that little light...keep shining bright!

That little poem contains so much truth. When a little light enters a large dark room, even the vast amount of darkness can't extinguish it. The darkness is always overcome by the light. At times I felt that all of the darkness in the world was pressing in on me. Yet, it could never cover the light of Jesus in my heart.

Each of us is called to be a light shining in the darkness of this world. Fear God and not man. Don't be ashamed of the Gospel of Christ. We are debtors, and we owe it to the world to proclaim the Gospel of Christ Jesus.

PART TWO

CHAPTER

6

GOD'S RESTORATION

When I first met Jesus, I was terrified when I realized that I could have gone to hell. Now that I have grown in the knowledge of God, I'm terrified that others will go to hell. With all of my being I beg you to make heaven and miss hell. The following pages of this book will show you how to do that.

Hebrews 4:15,16 says, *For we have not an high priest which cannot be touched with the feeling of our infirmities; but was in all points tempted like as we are, yet without sin. Let us therefore come boldly unto the throne of grace, that we may obtain mercy, and find grace to help in time of need.*

Jesus, the Son of God, came to Earth in flesh and blood as a man. He was tempted as we are. Because of that, He knows firsthand about hunger, pain, disappointment and anything else we might experience. But, because Jesus is also God, He knows us more than we will ever know ourselves. He has compassion upon us, and He floods us with grace and mercy in our time of need.

Jesus has been touched with the feelings of our infirmities. I felt alone and rejected all my life. Likewise, Jesus went to court and stood before Pilate <u>alone</u> (Matthew 27:2). All of His followers abandoned Him and denied Him. The very people who had sung His praises a few days earlier now rejected Him screaming, "Crucify Him!" Jesus knew loneliness and rejection. He came to earth to save us, yet most refused to follow and accept His salvation. Even those who saw miracles take place through His hands wouldn't believe.

When my broken voice called out to Him for help, His mercy flowed because He had "been there" Himself. We may not fully understand it, but His heart is tender toward us. I want you to know that no matter what you've done, you can call upon Him, and when you do, you will find an understanding Savior full of compassion and love. That is why I turned to Jesus.

I had ignored Him throughout my entire life. Almost every decision that I had ever made was contrary to His Word. That rebellion against God resulted in the devastation and upheaval in my life. I had nothing to offer God, so why would He want me? You might be asking that same question: Why would the God of the Universe, the One who made everything, want me? My life was so broken. My mind was such a mess. No one else wanted me. You may feel the same way.

The good news is that God knows you are a sinner. In fact, the worst thing that you have ever done doesn't shock Him! He is aware of every sin that you have ever committed, and He loves you in spite of your sin. The Bible says, "But God commendeth his love toward us, in that, while we were yet sinners, Christ died for us" (Romans 5:8). He died so that you could be rescued from your sin! In spite of all that I had done and all the mistakes that I had made, Jesus called my name. He came into that prison to claim me as His own. When I responded to His call, He began a process of healing in me.

Right now, ask yourself this question, "Does Jesus want me?" You must realize that Jesus' answer to that question is a resounding "YES!" He loves you, and He cares for you. When Jesus was here on Earth, He often irritated the noble and respected people by reaching out to sinners. There are so many instances of that in the Bible. One example takes place in the book of John chapter 8. Jesus stood up for a woman caught in the very act of adultery. At that time, adultery was a capital offense. Had Jesus not been there that day, the woman would have been stoned to death. The popular thing for Jesus to have done when the woman was brought to Him would have been to pick up a stone and join the crowd. But Jesus' response was different. He told the crowd that the person who was sinless could throw the first stone at the woman. Everyone in the crowd knew that they had each sinned, so one by one the stones began to drop to the ground as the crowd dispersed silently. The woman was not the only sinner in that town that day, you see. Jesus had revealed their sins also. Finally, after the last stone had fallen away, He was alone with the woman. At that point Jesus uttered some of the most beautiful words ever spoken. "Woman, where are those thine accusers?" He asked. "Neither do I condemn thee: go, and sin no more" (John 8:10,11). I love those words. They show the heart of God toward not only that woman, but to all mankind. That same merciful God came to me in prison. He didn't come to condemn me, I was already condemned. No, Jesus came to reach out to me, to stand with me, to befriend me, to save me. He washed away my sins and all of the guilt that I had carried throughout my life. I know the Jesus who stood with that woman; I met Him too, in prison. He stood with me just like He stood with her. Everyone else turned from the woman. She was a complete outcast. The only one who stood with her was Jesus. The only one who stood with me was Jesus.

People have different weaknesses, different flaws, and different backgrounds. In the Bible there are many examples of Jesus' tender mercy and love for all sorts of people. Mary Magdalene was possessed with seven demons before she met Jesus (Luke 8:2); the apostle Paul was a killer who persecuted the church (Acts 7:58; Acts 8:1); Matthew a tax collector (Matthew 10:3); Luke a doctor (Colossians 4:14); Nicodemus a Jewish leader (John 3:1). These were all different kinds of people, but they had one thing in common: Jesus wanted each one of them as His own.

II Peter 3:9 tells us that, "The Lord is. . .not willing that any should perish, but that all should come to repentance." Jesus wants you! He cares for you. He's calling to you. Accept Him as your Savior and Lord. He won't turn you away. He'll welcome you with open arms.

After I got a Bible from the prison chaplain's office, I started reading the New Testament. Many Scriptures became precious to me. I loved the wisdom that I found in them. They were a guide for me to follow. They instructed me on how to live and act. I was in prison, and there was nothing else to do, so I read the Bible over and over again. One of my favorite Scriptures was Matthew 11:28-30 when Jesus said,

Come unto me, all ye that labor and are heavy laden, and I will give you rest. Take my yoke upon you, and learn of me; for I am meek and lowly in heart: and ye shall find rest unto your souls. For my yoke is easy and my burden is light.

The heart of God is clearly shown in that verse. He calls the weak, weary, and downtrodden to Himself. I definitely qualified as a weak and weary soul; I needed to find rest and peace in my heart.

Another passage of Scripture that became very special to me was the account of the life of Joseph in Genesis chapters 39 through 50. Joseph's brothers sold him into slavery. Through a series of events, he ended up in prison—but God did not leave him there. One day he was a prisoner and the next day he was Prime Minister of Egypt. I liked that story because it gave me hope. If God could do that with Joseph's life, maybe He could do something with mine.

Overall, prison was no fun. It was often frightening and unpredictable. However, it was great to see God take care of me through the trials of prison life. I learned to trust Him. What a place to learn to lean on Jesus! In prison, you have no control over anything. So I quickly learned to pray and then trust Jesus for the outcome. On the street, or in everyday life, people pray and then interfere in the matter. In prison there is no way for you to interfere; you are forced to be patient.

I can't explain the workings of God. I don't know how God takes a prisoner, changes his heart, removes his old nature, and changes his nature to be like His own. But I know that the more I read, prayed and trusted God, the more my life improved. My mind became clearer and clearer until I was seeing everything in a new light.

As I studied the Bible, I learned three basic steps for growing closer to Jesus. If you want to get close and stay close to Jesus, each day you must:

1. Read and study the Bible.
2. Pray. Spend time talking to the Father and listening to His voice.
3. Fellowship (hang out) with other believers.

Those three little steps will keep you in tune with the Father. You will become sensitive to His leading and guidance. When you make a mistake, His Spirit will correct you and lead you into all truth. These steps are simple, yet they are the life-lines through which the power of God flows to His children. Cut out any one of these steps, and you cut your direct line to the Father. Keep the lines open, and everything good will come from the Father. "Every good gift and every perfect gift is from above, and cometh down from the Father of lights, with whom is no variableness, neither shadow of turning" (James 1:17).

CHAPTER

7

REBUILDING LIFE

A popular misconception about prison is that it functions to rehabilitate convicts. Most rational people would admit that doesn't actually happen; yet the belief is perpetuated by the prison system. Even the word "rehabilitate" proves that it can't happen. The word rehabilitate means to return to a former, better condition. That can never happen with most convicts. I shoplifted at age five. I did burglaries in seventh grade and began drug use in eighth grade. My first Class X felony conviction came at age seventeen. I was arrested for five more felonies, convicted and sent to prison at age eighteen. How would it have been possible for me to return to a former, better condition? I did not have a former, better condition. Obviously, this wasn't possible. There was never a "'golden age" to which I could return.[1] That's why most rehabilitation programs are such failures. Usually there is not much inherent good in the person being "rehabilitated." Yet, counselors try unsuccessfully to make the prisoners into something they never were. It is a formula destined to fail.

With Jesus, the approach is totally different. The Bible teaches that each person is born with a "sin

---

[1] This point is well stated by Allen Manske in an article titled, "Rehabilitation or Regeneration," printed in Logo's publication; **The Crack in the Wall.**

nature" (Romans 6:17). We are inherently sinful. Each person has sinned and therefore is worthy of death (Romans 3:23; 6:23). When we accept Jesus as our Savior, He takes our sin away and casts it into the depths of the sea (Micah 7:19). The Bible says that when we are in Christ, or saved, we are new creatures. *"Therefore if any man be in Christ, he is a new creature: old things are passed away; behold, all things are become new"* (2 Corinthians 5:17). Jesus doesn't try to rebuild the old house. He bulldozes the old one down so that he can build a mansion where the shack once stood. So it is for each of us. Coming to Jesus means that there is a newness to our lives. After all, it is called being "born again." It's a brand new start (John 3:3).

As soon as you ask Jesus to forgive you of your sins and to come into your heart and be your Savior and Lord, you are saved. Your spirit is born again (John 3). Unfortunately, your mind is the same old filthy mind you always had. My mind was filled with eighteen years of pain, hurt, sin, and hatred.

The Bible says that we are to renew our minds by the washing of water by the word (Ephesians 5:26). By reading the Bible, you begin to replace your carnal thoughts with God's thoughts. Your thoughts got you into your present mess. God's thoughts will keep you from getting into trouble (Romans 12:2). Here are some examples of God's thoughts versus your thoughts.

Your thought: I think I'll steal this stereo and sell it for cash.

Result: You are caught and end up in prison or with a hefty fine.

God's thought: "Let him that stole steal no more: but rather let him labor, working with his hands the thing which is good, that he may have to give to him that needeth" (Ephesians 4:28).

Result: You get a job, learn a trade, work hard and become a productive citizen in society. Then, when you see people in need, you have money to help them. By doing this, you step outside of your selfish nature into a higher realm—where you care for your fellow man. Your life takes on new value. Once you've tasted it, you'll never go back!

Your thought: Things aren't going too well. I think I'm going to buy a case of beer and get toasted.

Result: You get toasted. While your brain is in neutral, Satan, your enemy, talks you into doing something stupid and destructive. You wake up broke and miserable.

God's thought: "And be not drunk with wine, wherein is excess; but be filled with the Spirit" (Ephesians 5:18).

Result: You are sober and filled with the Spirit of God. You can think rationally. Satan can't talk you into doing something stupid. God takes hold of your heart and begins to touch you deeply. You begin to mature as a Christian. Now you've experienced the goodness of God.

Your thought: Whoa baby, check out that good lookin' little momma over there. My wife is gone; she'll never know. I'll ask this babe out for a good time!

Result: The devil can't keep a secret. Your wife finds out, and you break her heart. You're too proud to admit that you were wrong. You get into a big fight and you lose your precious wife.

God's thought: "Let thy fountain be blessed: and rejoice with the wife of thy youth. Let her be as thy loving hind and pleasant roe; let her breasts satisfy thee at all times; and be thou ravished always with her love" (Proverbs 5:18,19).

Result: That's right, Casanova, spend the money you were going to spend on "little miss devil's trap," on your wife instead. Be satisfied with her. God will bless you. You'll begin to have a stronger relationship with her because you're hanging in with God.

Your thought: I don't need a job. I can draw unemployment for another six months. Then, when that runs out, I can apply for the federal extension.

Result: You are not learning a trade, not earning your way, and not growing as a person. Idle hand's are the devil's workshop, as they say. True! You have too much time on your hands and you get into trouble. Before you know it you are back into your old habits.

God's thought: "For even when we were with you,

this we commanded you, that if any would not work, neither should he eat" (II Thessalonians 3:10).

"But if any provide not for his own, and specially for those of his own house, he hath denied the faith, and is worse than an infidel"(I Timothy 5:8).

Result: You get a job. God blesses your efforts. You work hard, and are promoted. You learn to be trustworthy, and faithful. God sees your efforts at work. His blessings come into your life. Your family respects you and you respect yourself. Your life is changing.

One of the most important things on the road to a new life is W-O-R-K! If you can't find a job, look every day, all day. Don't waste your time watching TV. Don't hang out with your friends. Get a job! If you have to, go to the local grocery store and sweep the floors for free, but work. If you have to work for weeks with no pay—do it. Get a job and stick with it. At the end of a hard day, Jesus will walk home with you. You'll look into the mirror and see a man (or woman) of integrity looking back at you. How rewarding!

I could go on and on with examples, but you get the idea. The Bible is the Word of God. It is spirit, and it is life. As you read the Bible, you will cleanse your mind from all of the lies of this world. When you read the Bible, you replace your thoughts with God's thoughts. With God's thoughts, you grow, mature and begin to live the way you were created to live—in victory! There is comfort and peace when you live for God. Ephesians 6:17 says, *"And take the helmet of salvation, and the sword of the Spirit, which is the word of God: praying always with all prayer and supplications in the Spirit."*

I encourage you to read the Bible with all of the strength you have. Place the Word of God into your heart. Joshua 1:8 says,

This book of the law shall not depart out of thy mouth; but thou shalt meditate herein day and night, that thou mayest observe to do according to all that is written therein: for then thou shalt make thy way prosperous, and then thou shalt have good success.

Before I knew those Scriptures, I'd never studied or meditated on God's Word. As a result I was a rebellious, hateful, and confused man. To many, studying the Bible may not seem too exciting, but how do you know? What if the Bible brings stability, encouragement, guidance, and peace into your life? What if it helps free you from habits that have held you captive for years? What if it is actually alive and supernaturally brings the life of God into your heart and mind? Think for a moment about the meaning of these Scriptures.

Matthew 24:35: *Heaven and earth shall pass away, but my words shall not pass away.*

John 6:63: *(Jesus said:) It is the spirit that quickeneth (brings us life); the flesh profiteth nothing: the words that I speak unto you, they are spirit, and they are life.*

John 8:31,32: *Then said Jesus. . .If ye continue in my word, then are ye my disciples indeed; and ye shall know the truth, and the truth shall make you free.*

Isaiah 55:11: *So shall my word be that goeth forth out of my mouth: it shall not return unto me void, but it shall accomplish that which I please, and it shall prosper in the thing whereto I sent it.*

At this writing, twenty four years later, I can wholeheartedly attest to the fact that what I've said is true. Meditating on the Word of God does make you prosper and have good success. Nothing in my life has ever made me successful, except Jesus and His precious Word (Joshua 1:8). Devour it daily.

CHAPTER

8

FIGHTING THE BATTLE

Living for Jesus is a battle. There is an old hymn that states, "I'm in the Lord's army." How true! It is safe to say that no one will get to heaven without a fight. As Christians, the three major foes that we fight are Satan, our flesh, and the world.

<u>Satan</u>

In John 10:10 Jesus says, "The thief cometh not, but for to steal, and to kill, and to destroy: I am come that they might have life, and that they might have it more abundantly." The thief in this passage is clearly the devil, also called Satan. Yes, he is real, and he comes to steal, to kill, and to destroy. Your foe is now identified once and for all—it's Satan. It isn't the cops, the system, your husband, your wife, or any man; the foe that you are fighting is the devil.

The Bible tells us that Satan was once an angel, and that with some other angels tried to exalt himself above God. As a result, he and those other angels, now called demons, were banished from heaven forever. There is no redemption for Satan or any other angel who rebelled. Their destiny is eternity in hell. There is no escaping that destiny. Satan hates God.

Here is where humans come into play: You were made in the image of God (Gen. 1:26). Therefore,

Satan hates you with the same intensity he hates God. Satan cannot harm God in any way, but he can get at humanity. Stealing, killing, and destroying the human race is Satan's hell-bent passion. His hatred toward us is beyond our most vile imagination. His goal is to drag us with him into everlasting separation from God (hell). Once we are there, he will torment us for eternity; he will torment us because we walked away from the gift of eternal life with our loving Father God.

On a number of occasions I have overheard people nonchalantly announce that they were going to hell "because all of my friends are there." Do those people realize that hell is the worst place ever created in the universe? Nothing that has ever existed can compare with the misery, pain, and torment that is contained therein. There are no "friends" in hell. Hatred rules. The very demons that convinced hell's occupants to go there will turn on them and torment them for eternity. Those deceived people could have gone to heaven by accepting Jesus as their Savior, but instead, they chose hell. The torment will never end.

Our enemy is further defined in Ephesians 6:12,13, *For we wrestle not against flesh and blood, but against principalities, against powers, against the rulers of the darkness of this world, against spiritual wickedness in high places. Wherefore take unto you the whole armor of God, that ye may be able to withstand in the evil day, and having done all, to stand.*

You may want to further study the whole armor of God in Ephesians 6:14-19. God has given us powerful weapons to use in our warfare against the devil, but it's up to us to pick those weapons up and learn how to use them. The three main weapons mentioned in the Bible are the Word of God (the Bible), the Name of Jesus, and the Blood of Jesus.

In Luke 4:3-13, Jesus had been praying and fasting in the desert for forty days. At His weakest moment, Satan came to tempt Him. Three times Satan tempted Him, and each time, Jesus turned the temptation away by quoting Scripture. Repeatedly Jesus answered, "It is written. . ." If Jesus used the Scriptures to defeat Satan, then so should we. That is all the more reason to hide the Word of God in our hearts and minds. We study the Bible so that we, too, can say, "It is written. . ." We can't say that if we haven't placed God's Word in our hearts, because we won't know what is written. Luke 4:1-4 tells us,

Then Jesus being full of the Holy Ghost returned from Jordan, and was led by the Spirit into the wilderness, being forty days tempted of the devil. And in those days he did eat nothing: and when they were ended, he afterward hungered. And the devil said unto him, If thou be the Son of God, command this stone that it be made bread. And Jesus answered him, saying, It is written, That man shall not live by bread alone, but by every word of God.

Luke 22:31 says, *And the Lord said, Simon, Simon, behold, Satan hath desired to have you, that he may sift you as wheat: But I have prayed for thee that thy faith fail not: and when thou art converted, strengthen thy brethren.*

In this passage, Jesus told Peter, also called Simon, that Satan has plans to sift, or crush his life. Jesus prevented Satan from harming his friend Peter by praying for him. Prayer stopped Satan from destroying Peter. Peter was able to fulfill the plan that God had for his life through Jesus' prayer. How many times have we let Satan sift us or our friends as wheat by not praying? Prayer clearly stops Satan's attacks.

Our prayers have power because of the blood that Jesus shed on the cross. I Peter 1:18,19 says,
Forasmuch as ye know that ye were not redeemed with corruptible things, as silver and gold. . .but with the precious blood of Christ, as of a lamb without blemish and without spot.

We can stop the enemy with the Word of God, with prayer in the Name of Jesus, and with the Blood of Jesus. By using these weapons we can stop Satan from stealing, killing, and destroying our lives in the present and in the future. When you pray, do so in the Name of Jesus. Petition the Lord to work in your behalf according to His perfect will. Remember, only He knows what is best for you!

Our Flesh

We are spirit beings housed inside a body of flesh, blood, and bones. When we accept Jesus, our spirit becomes alive. Our spirit is eternal, and when it comes alive to God, it wants to rule our lives. But, as newborn spirit beings, we have a weak spirit because for so long we have starved it. Likewise, our flesh is strong because for so many years it has been indulged and fed. We pamper our flesh. If it's hungry, we feed it. If it's tired, we put it to bed. My flesh wanted drugs, so I gave it drugs. The list goes on and on. Our flesh dominates our existence. It does have natural needs: food, water and protection from the elements of weather, but often times it also becomes the part of us that craves sin and other unhealthy pleasure. Most Americans spend their entire lives serving their flesh.

Our flesh is at war with our spirit. Our spirit longs to be like Jesus; in fact, when Jesus communicates with us, He does it through our spirit. As our spirit grows, we become more in tune with the Holy Spirit. We have a greater sense of God's presence in our lives. The Word tells us that those who are led by the Spirit, are the sons of God. That's why Jesus said that we are to take up our cross and follow Him daily. Crosses only have one purpose, and that is to crucify the flesh. "I am crucified with Christ: nevertheless I live. . ." (Galatians 2:20). We are to deny our flesh daily so that God's Spirit can commune with our spirit.

When I first accepted Christ the idea of denying my flesh was foreign to me. As a drug addict and dealer, my entire existence was based upon serving my flesh. In fact, satisfying my flesh was a full time job. I satisfied it with drugs, alcohol, sex, food and whatever else it desired. Denying my flesh was not easy! One day I read in the Bible about fasting and praying. Jesus told His disciples that a certain kind of demon came out only by prayer and fasting (Mark 9:29). If fasting was a key to getting closer to Jesus, I wanted to try it. I decided to fast for the entire month of March. For thirty-one days, I didn't eat. I prayed and turned my heart toward God. I denied my flesh to strengthen my spiritual man. It may seem extreme, but fasting taught me that I could control my body. It was crying out for food, but I didn't have to feed it. It wanted drugs, but I didn't have to give in. Years of my life were being changed by the power of God. I knew that without a change, I'd be in prison for the rest of my life, so I wanted all the change I could get!

I remember one situation that took place after my release from prison in which some Christian friends talked to me about changing certain areas of my life. They were right, and I knew it, but their corrections angered me. I threw them out of my house! After they left, I sat there, feeling miserable inside. My flesh had gotten me into trouble, again. There was a decision to make, and I knew that if I didn't submit to their correction, I'd be lost. It was a life and death decision for me. As an ex-drug dealer, I was used to running the show. This time I couldn't do that. I went to the Christian friends, repented, asked their forgiveness and received their correction. My proud flesh didn't like it, but my flesh is what had led me to prison, and I didn't want to go back. Our relationship was healed, and I'm still friends with them today, over twenty years later.

The World

Look around you. Everywhere you look, your eyes are bombarded with a thousand messages a day. "Buy this, and you'll get a girl that looks like that." "Drive this car, and show the world that you're a success." "Act like this; think like this." "This is cool; this is not." "Those shoes are out of style; these are in." "Success looks like this; failure looks like that." From aftershave to money market funds—from Wall Street to Skid Row, we are constantly given information. That is the world!

One side of the world's message is the "finer things of life" message. It's a confused system of greed, lust, striving, wanting and no ultimate satisfaction—it's "upper crust." It's a guy with a Mercedes dreaming of a Rolls Royce. It's thinking that the next purchase, accomplishment or conquest will bring that longed for satisfaction. It's the lie that all is well because you've got cash. It's thinking that you're just a little bit better than the next man because your house is bigger and you have more money. It's wanting to be well thought of and respected. Cash and luxury won't save you. Longing for more of the things of this world is an empty, lonely existence. In such a state, you're just as hopeless as a poor, hopeless wino who has bought a different lie of the world. Wealth without Jesus is just a different kind of poverty. Song writer Bob Bennett wrote a song called "Beggar." One line of the songs says, "We all know how it feels to be starving in the heart." How true. It's poverty of spirit. That's the world.

In the Bible, there was a rich man who died and

went to hell. From hell, the rich man begged Abraham for two things. The first was a drop of water for his scorched tongue, and the second was that someone be sent to his father's house to warn his five brothers about hell. The requests were denied. His brothers had many witnesses to the existence of God, yet they ignored them. The rich man had been a prince of the world, yet he lost everything (Luke 16).

This world lies. Everything that the world offers is a lie. The Bible calls this deception the lust of this world, the pride of life, the deceitfulness of riches and the cares of this world. The world promotes carnal things, but ridicules Christianity and morality. The world portrays Christians in the most negative ways possible. When was the last time you saw a Christian portrayed in a positive light in a movie or on TV? It does not happen very often.

Thirty-nine members of a cult in California committed suicide in an attempt to meet a space ship that they believed was following the Hale-Bopp comet. Following this tragedy, not one news report spoke negatively about the views of the leader who convinced his followers to kill themselves. The media treated him with sensitivity and respect. Why? The answer is simple: A group of UFO followers doesn't bring *conviction* to the world *of its sin*. Thus, reporters weren't offended by the cult's beliefs. Jesus, however, is offensive to many people because He convicts the world of its lost state and reminds the people of their impending doom if they reject Him. Because of this conviction, the world persecutes Christians verbally, socially and physically. Typically, if a Christian makes the smallest mistake, the media broadcasts it over and over again in an attempt to silence those who dare to speak the truth about Jesus.

Furthermore, this world is not only cruel to those who follow Christ's guidelines for living, but it is cruel to those who follow the world's own guidelines for living. Countless movie stars, musicians, business people, executives and writers have climbed the ladder of success only to find that "the top" was a lonely, miserable existence. Suicide has been the solution to many people who "had it all." The world system uses people and then discards them.

Many times we've heard of famous people, once adored by millions, left standing alone in bankruptcy. When the money is gone, the mansion is gone, and the "friends" are gone, what remains?

The drug culture encourages the "druggies" to take more pills, shoot more stuff, snort more stuff, and drink more stuff. It's always "just a little more." The result of drug abuse is destroyed minds. Drugged out people have trouble identifying social situations, and can barely carry on normal conversions. They are called "burn outs" or labeled as being "fried." "Burn outs" are laughed at, humiliated and hassled by others in the drug world. The derogatory term "burn out" wasn't coined by bankers or doctors; it came from the drug culture. How cruel. These people obey the "laws" of their society and it destroys their mind. Then the society of "friends" turns on them and labels them "burn outs." They end up as a joke in their own subculture.

The same thing happens with girls and sex. Messages that encourage youths to have sex are everywhere. Schools even pass out condoms! Many advertisements, prime time TV shows, rock songs, movies and billboards encourage teenage girls to have sex. If a girl gives in to the message, then she is labeled as "loose" or "easy." If she does not then she is a "prude." Even the boyfriend who swore his love to her and promised he'd never leave will turn on her. One day she is his girlfriend whom he'd never leave; the next she is the subject of a juicy locker-room story.

If there is a pregnancy, the poor girl will give birth alone. When the baby begins to develop, and she gains some weight, the boyfriend "discovers" that perhaps he didn't love her after all. While she cries out in labor pains, he will be cruising Main Street looking for a new girlfriend. The world's system wastes lives.

I'm reminded of my friend Teresa who died during childbirth at age seventeen. Her boyfriend never shed a tear. He just partied on.

Another time a girl I knew had an abortion while her boyfriend drove around St. Louis and smoked pot with his buddy. That boyfriend never felt a thing! A week later she was curled up on the couch in a spasm and couldn't move. They rushed her back to the clinic. The doctor hadn't gotten all of the baby out. Body parts were rotting inside her, and she was being poisoned by the decay. She underwent an excruciatingly painful procedure to remove the rest of the baby. Again, the boyfriend drove around and smoked pot. He didn't feel a thing. That girl was completely alone. Her mom wasn't even there to help her.

The list of satan's traps goes on for eternity. The message is clear: this world and its values lead to death. The Bible calls Satan the god of this world. This world is hard and cold. It does not care about you. You can follow the world's instructions but the result will always be destruction, heartache, pain, tears and misery.

Everything that this world has to offer is urging you on, luring you into sin. While you obey the world, you are the life of the party—but eventually the wages of sin is death. When the destruction of sin hits your life, you'll be alone. Totally alone. As a drug dealer, I thought I was on top of the world. But my "friends" disappeared when I was arrested. When I walked through the prison door, no friends were with me. I was completely alone. Ultimately, when you stand before Jesus at judgment, you will be alone. No one will stand with you. You, and you alone, will account for what you have done (Acts 17:31).

Jesus isn't like those you may consider to be your friends now. He said, "I will never leave thee, nor forsake thee" (Hebrews 13:5). And, "There is a friend that sticketh closer than a brother" (Proverbs 18:24). This life is full of trials, and Jesus will go through every one of them with you when you ask Him into your heart.

I pray to God that I can stop just one person from getting to know this world and the heartache, pain and anguish that go along with it. The tree that Adam and Eve couldn't eat from, in the Garden, contained the knowledge of good and evil. Man was not created to know evil, that is why God did not want Adam and Eve to eat from that tree. Yes, Jesus heals people like me—who have tasted the fruit of evil, but the toll that sin took on my life was very great. I've experienced so much heartache as a result of sin. There are things I cannot even write about because they're so offensive. Ask yourself this: Who is smarter, the person who injures himself through reckless behavior and is then saved through a major operation by a great doctor, or the person who sees the danger, avoids it and never needs that major surgery? Obviously, the person who avoids danger is smarter. Thank God that when I needed the operation He was there, but my desire is to see that you never need the operation. Please don't make the mistakes that I did.

If you are young and have not given in to this world, I beg you not to. Turn your eyes upon Jesus. He is merciful, kind, loving and full of compassion. He loves you so much. His plan for you is for you to be blessed. Save your heart from the misery of this world. Call upon Jesus every day. Don't sin against Him. Love Him, and He will bless your life.

After my release from prison, I joined a church where I taught the youth Sunday school class and Wednesday night Bible studies. After getting to know and love the members of the class, I wrote this poem for them:

Youth Song
Don't let anyone despise your youth
your hearts are full of God and you know the truth
The life in front of you will be so complete
If you serve your God and know His peace
Just serve your God and know His peace.

Though you are young, certainly you have a foe
Satan greatly desires to take control
though you are opposed, still you'll be blessed
Serve your God and know His rest
Oh, serve your God and know His rest.

I know the strengths and weaknesses in each of you
I have this heartfelt confidence you'll make it through
and I really love you so
I just wanted to let you know...

Don't let anyone despise your youth
your hearts are full of God and you know the truth
The life in front of you will be so complete
Just serve your God and know His peace
Just serve your God and know His peace.

But for some of us, Satan has already stolen part of our life. In my life, he stole years from me. What about those years? Joel 2: 25,26 says,

And I will restore to you the years that the locust hath eaten, the cankerworm, and the caterpillar, and the palmerworm, my great army which I sent among you. And ye shall eat in plenty, and be satisfied, and

praise the name of the Lord your God, that hath dealt wondrously with you: and my people shall never be ashamed.

In this passage, God promises to restore the years that were stolen by the enemy. When restoration occurs we can eat in plenty, be satisfied and praise God who deals wondrously with us. I assure you that God can and will restore to you all that was lost. He can return loved ones, jobs, homes, money and more. Satan may have won a few battles, but the war is not over yet! Through Jesus, you can stop Satan's attack and recover all that was lost.

So, if you have made some mistakes, ask Jesus to forgive and cleanse you. Then stop making those mistakes. If your "friends" are causing you to do things that you know you shouldn't do, get new friends. This may seem hard, but living in this world without Jesus is even harder.

Today, ask Jesus to begin the restoration process in you. Jesus did it for me, and He'll do it for you also. James 4:4 says, "Ye adulterers and adulteresses, know ye not that the friendship of the world is enmity with God? whosoever therefore will be a friend of the world is the enemy of God."

CHAPTER

9

SIN

As I read my Bible and talked with other Christians I became aware that my life was filled with sin. Then one day I read Ephesians 4:29,30:

Let no corrupt communication proceed out of your mouth, but that which is good to the use of edifying, that it may minister grace unto the hearers. And grieve not the holy Spirit of God, whereby ye are sealed unto the day of redemption.

Before I met Jesus, everything that came from my life was corrupt, but I did not care. Then I accepted Jesus. I prayed and read my Bible, and as I did, the Holy Spirit began to move in my heart. He began to convict me of my sins. When I sinned, my conscience bothered me. Sin began to *feel* bad. I knew when I did something wrong. I knew that some of my behavior was going to have to change if I was ever going to let Jesus heal my life. It amazed me that my actions could grieve the Holy Spirit. I did not want to grieve the Holy Spirit; I wanted to put sin out from my life. Sin led me to prison. I wanted to end its influence in my life.

Wanting to rid my life of sin may seem like an old-fashioned desire. Today's world views the Bible and the very idea of sin and holiness with a certain degree of contempt. If it isn't viewed with outright hostility, it's viewed with a mocking arrogance. "Really," the world cries out, "who could believe some of the stories in the Bible? For example: Adam and Eve in the Garden? How quaint." You can hear the modern world laughing at these notions every day. "How silly." The TV and billboards scream, "Death and destruction entered the world through a little sin? Sure. What does the Bible know? A little sin won't hurt anyone."

This modern world is much too sophisticated to believe such "stories." Yet, if this modern world would only read the newspapers and watch the evening news with some spiritual discernment, they'd see that sin destroys lives. Sin is still wreaking havoc. Sin is still bringing death. Destruction is still brought into lives today through the deadly force of sin.

Sin can take a millionaire doctor and leave him penniless. After one episode in sin the house can be gone, the Mercedes—gone, the art collection—gone, the wife and children—gone, everything—gone. Why? Perhaps it was just one "toke" of crack cocaine, one lucky night at the race track, or one tempting glance by a young, attractive person. Sin grabs you so that you can't let go!

Countless rock stars have "had it all" one day, only to wake up with nothing the next. What happened? Sin.

Sin will cause a man to leave his wife and children to fend for themselves. It will cause a child to murder his entire family. Sin turns a precious young girl with hopes and dreams into merchandise for any man with the highest bid. Sin turns little boys into killers, little girls into drug addicts, bank presidents into thieves, and professional ball players into panhandlers. Sin is the most destructive force in the universe. Satan uses sin to put mankind into bondage. At first sin is fun. The Bible tells us that (Hebrews 11:25). It also tells us that eventually the sin controls the sinner (Romans 6). He (or she) becomes a slave to sin.

The more that we give in to sin, the more it is established as our master. The more it is established as our master, the stronger it becomes in our lives. Sin is a taskmaster like no other. It forces those who serve it to do things they would have never done. Eventually sin leads to the death of the sinner (Romans 6:21). Sin doesn't destroy the sinner just once in a while. It does it each and every time! No person who has ever walked on this earth has been able to control sin. Sin will rule the heart and life of any man *who will let it. However,* Jesus is excluded; He never sinned.

Do you remember the words of Jesus when He warned Peter, "Simon, Simon, behold, Satan hath desired to have you, that he may sift you as wheat" (Luke 22:31)? Sin grinds a person into nothing. It leaves people weak, powerless and empty. Why does sin enslave us so? The answer is simple. Mankind was not made to serve sin. We were made in the image of God (Genesis 9:6). We were designed to love and obey God. Our beings were never created to suffer under the weight of sin. Here are some scriptures concerning sin:

Ephesians 5:3-5, *But fornication, and all uncleanness, or covetousness, let it not be once named among you, as becometh saints; neither filthiness, nor foolish talking, nor jesting, which are not convenient: but rather giving of thanks. For this ye know, that no whoremonger, nor unclean person, nor covetous man, who is an idolater, hath any inheritance in the kingdom of Christ and of God.*

Romans 1:29-32, *Being filled with all unrighteousness, fornication, wickedness, covetousness, maliciousness; full of envy, murder, debate, deceit, malignity; whisperers, backbiters, haters of God, despiteful, proud, boasters, inventors of evil things, disobedient to parents, without understanding, covenantbreakers, without natural affection, implacable, unmerciful: who knowing the judgment of God, that they which commit such things are worthy of death, not only do the same, but have pleasure in them that do them.*

It is for these reasons that the Bible repeatedly warns us to flee from sin. It isn't that God is a spoil-sport who doesn't know how to have a good time. He loves us, and therefore, doesn't want us to do things that will result in death. He's there warning us as loud as He can. Those who hear His voice and obey will be spared the destruction of sin. Those who disobey and rebelliously sin bear the results of their actions. He has given us a free will with which to obey or disobey—to choose life or death.

Here are a number of examples of people I personally know whose lives have been destroyed by sin:

1. I knew a successful lawyer who set up trust funds for many families. He worked for a major law firm and was well respected, but he started gambling. His losses were so great that in desperation he spent all of the money in the trust funds before he was finally discovered. In a matter of months he went from being a respected attorney to being a hated felon. He received a sentence of ten years in prison.

2. As a young salesman, I called on a company that appeared on the surface to be phenomenally successful. They were in a new office and drove new vehicles—and everything was first class. The owner was twenty-five and drove a brand new Rolls Royce Silver Cloud. Within three years he was in federal prison. He was a gambler; he gambled and lost. To cover his losses he forged a U.S. Post Office money order for $250,000.00. The feds caught him. He was convicted, but before they could ship him to prison, the mob caught up with him in jail and broke both of his legs for not paying a debt.

3. In my business I bought products from a company in the south. My supplier made so much money that he started a boat company to manufacture boats based upon a radical new design. The boats were a hit. He was on top of the world. Not too long afterward, however, he was arrested for sexually molesting his daughters. His case made the national news and was covered nightly by CNN news. He was found guilty and

received a life sentence. Five years later his wife was killed in a car wreck. They "had everything," yet sin destroyed their family.

Sin is an equal opportunity destroyer. It destroyed the lives of these successful people with the same efficiency it displayed on me and many others. Age, race, gender, and social strata are all irrelevant with sin. Sin destroys everyone equally, if given the chance. But here is a clue: Sin always starts with a thought and then grows until it is followed by an action. I wrote a poem to describe how sin starts small and then grows until it destroys. The poem is called "Sin's Progressive."

Sin's Progressive

Saw a man doing life in prison
and asked him how come
He said when I was five I stole bubble gum
then when I was six I stole candy bars
it was down hill from there, you know how kids are
At age 15 I was doing major jobs
all I ever did was steal some more and rob
At age 25 I had a gun in my hand
one job fell apart and I shot a man.

And I said, "Sin's progressive!"

Saw an alcoholic there, he's in the detox room
He's sweating and shaking,

screaming death's coming soon
He said I started drinking on the weekends
and it really was fun
but soon I stopped waiting
for those weekends to come
I started drinking whiskey
now I drink aftershave or Listerine™
anything to take the pain away
those detox blues sure get mean
I never thought it'd be this way when I was young
and drunk and having fun
I never thought I'd be a alky in a detox center
wishing death would come.

And I said, "Sin's progressive!"

You probably think that little sin's leading nowhere
But oh don't you know that little sin
is the pathway to the devil's snare
he's trying to ruin your life
he's trying to steal your husband or your wife
he's out to rob steal and kill
he wants to make you a captive of his will.

Young man, broken marriage
got his eyes full of tears
he'd give the universe and more
just to hold his baby near
he left her, she left him
and it all grew out of one little sin
he looked into a lady's eyes

not realizing it was Satan's snare there in disguise
it took a tragedy for that poor boy to realize
sin's progressive.

Your probably think that little sin's leading nowhere
But oh don't you know that little sin
is the pathway to the devil's snare
he's trying to ruin your life
he's trying to steal your husband or your wife
he's out to rob steal and kill
he wants to make you a captive of his will.

You can stop the power of sin in your life today. You can wipe sin completely out of your life, right now! The steps are simple, but very powerful:

1. Jesus shed His blood as He died on the cross for our sins. That blood is the payment for all of the sins ever committed. Your sins were washed away by that blood at Calvary (Romans 3:24,25).

2. When Jesus died, He conquered death, hell, and the grave (Revelation 1:18). Therefore, sin doesn't have power over us when we choose to follow Jesus. Make a conscious effort to walk with Jesus daily, and you will conquer sin.

3. When you ask Jesus to come into your heart and to be your Savior, He washes away your sin. At that moment you are cleansed from all sin and are no longer a slave to it. Ask Him into your heart today!

4. The word the Bible uses to describe what we must do as we confess our sin to Jesus is "repent." That word means to turn away from, or to make an "about face" as a soldier does when he marches. You are going in one direction, you repent of your sins, and then turn completely around. You march in a totally different direction. You must stop doing the things that are keeping you from an intimate relationship with Jesus.

5. You recognize sin as your mortal enemy. You hate it; you despise it; you don't flirt with it anymore. You don't make eye contact with it. You avoid sin like the plague.

6. Once you have repented, begin to renew your mind with the Bible and seek God through prayer (Romans 12:2).

7. If there is a particular sin that you have been involved in for a period of time, it may have a strong grip on your life. You must realize that sin is your mortal enemy. It is trying to destroy you. Therefore, fight it with everything you have. Resist it. Command it to leave you in Jesus' Name. Do not quit fighting until that sin is no longer controlling you.

Too many Christians who have lived for Jesus forget the devastation that was associated with the sins of their past. Again, they slowly begin to entertain thoughts. Those thoughts, left unchecked, will lead to action. Soon those Christians find themselves in bondage to sin again. Sin in a Christian's life leads to the same death that it does in an unsaved person's life. Sin equals death every time.

We have to flee from sin. Please don't think that I'm exaggerating! Sin is your enemy! It WILL kill you! Fight it with all of your being! Never give in to it! Each time you give in to sin, you become weaker, and the sin becomes stronger. Each time you resist sin, you become stronger, and the sin becomes weaker. Resist!

The result of your struggle against sin will be a relationship with God unhindered by sin. Through this victory, you can freely have a relationship with God. Your prayers will be heard and answered. You can come to God without guilt. The Bible says that your body is a holy temple where the Holy Spirit resides (1 Corinthians 6:19). When sin rules in your body, it competes with God. When there is no sin, the Holy Spirit can live in you and through you freely and without hindrance. The Holy Spirit can teach you all truths. Sin brings on death, but a holy life filled with God brings life more abundantly.

CHAPTER

10

FORGIVENESS

Throughout my stay in prison, the subject that I heard most discussed was revenge. Every day, without exception, convicts talked about how they were going to get even with those on "the outside." They were going to get "the rat that narced on them," or they were going to get back at the cop who arrested them. They were going to terrorize the people who testified against them—on and on it went without end. Most convicts discuss hatred and revenge daily. This is one of the main reasons that prisoners go back to prison. It's simple. They get out, try to even the score, and in doing so end up back in prison. Then, there is more to hate, more scores to settle, and the cycle repeats itself.

God is not in the business of revisiting the past. He is the God of the NOW. Yesterday is not important to God. If it were important to God, we would have to constantly deal with our past. But that is not God's nature. Once we confess our sins and repent, God takes the past and throws it into the depths of the sea (Micah 7:19). He separates it from us like the east is from the west (Psalm 103:12). He washes it in the blood of His Son, Jesus. Furthermore, God doesn't want you to be guilty because of your past. He wants to forgive you, and He wants you to forgive yourself for your past. It's dead and gone, and it should be treated as such. When God forgives you of your past, you need to forget it. You can't drive a car by looking in the rearview mirror, and you can't run your life by looking to the past.

A big part of forgetting your past is forgiving all of those involved and asking them for their forgiveness. Forgive the cops, the witnesses, the jailers, the narcs. . .just forgive them all. Forgive your parents, your brothers and sisters—everyone who ever did you harm. Why? Because refusing to forgive chains you to your failures. The Bible says that we should forgive others as God has forgiven us. God also says that if you have unforgiveness toward someone, don't even pray with that dwelling in your heart. Go to the person, forgive him, and then pray (Mark 11:25).

Satan doesn't want you to be free from the past. He wants to keep you as a prisoner. When you forgive, you throw down the chains that once bound you. It's a wonderful feeling to let hatred go, to choose to release the hurts in your heart. Forgive all the people who have harmed you. Don't drag the pain around any longer. Then, and only then, can you be free from your past. When you get free from the past, the future starts to look bright.

Wherever you are, pray this prayer right now:

Lord Jesus, I forgive all those who have hurt me in the past. I forgive all those who helped put me where I am today. I forgive everyone who wanted to do me harm. I hold no anger toward them. I choose to forgive them right now. I ask You to touch their lives. I ask You to bless them. I ask You not to hold their sin against them.

I forgive them, Lord Jesus, and I ask You to forgive them, too. Jesus, let Your forgiveness fill my heart. Cleanse me from the past that I may never walk that way again. I give up my past to You, Jesus, so that You can bless my future. Touch me now, Lord Jesus. Let me walk in Your ways, Lord. Thank You for forgiving me of my sins as I have forgiven those that have sinned against me. In Your Name I pray, Amen."

I encourage you to pray that prayer every day. Forgiveness is an ongoing process. How many times must we forgive? Forever. Forgiveness is the key to the Kingdom of God. He forgave the world by sacrificing His only Son for us (John 3:16). We must forgive those in our world. Unforgiveness is truly a cancer. Never let it get hold of your heart. Forgive and you will always be free from the past. In my life, I forgave the police, the state's attorney, and even the kids who treated me badly when I was young. I forgave my dad for not being there, and I could go on and on. But with every act of forgiveness comes more and more freedom. Finally, now, the past has little effect on me. I am truly free from it.

Forgiveness is not an act of weakness. It is the exact opposite. Forgiveness is an act of character and of strength. When you forgive, you imitate God, and God's likeness is in you. That makes you strong. Unforgiveness makes you a slave to the past. Forgiveness sets you free. Let's get free, and let's stay free. We know what *we* made out of the past. Let's see what *God* can make out of our future.

CHAPTER

11

CHANGES

What you have just read is not fiction. Every word is true. The worst events of my life were omitted. I couldn't write about them because most people would find the stories too offensive.

You may ask yourself: Does living for Jesus really work? Does life improve? My answer is: Definitely! When I walked out of prison many years ago, no one gave me a chance of "making it." In prison, each inmate is assigned to a counselor. The counselors help the prisoners to cope with the many transitions that take place within the prison system. Before I left prison, my counselor told me that he knew I was a fake. He said that he could see through my "act." He predicted that I'd be back in six months and said that "he'd see me when I returned." He's still waiting. . .

Even the prison chaplain didn't believe in me. When I underwent the parole board review, he refused to write a recommendation for me saying that I had attended chapel regularly. Until then, I thought he was my friend. I realized that he didn't believe a word that I had said to him during our relationship. He thought that my entire presence at church was a charade.

No one expected me to succeed. The Bible says in I

Samuel 16:7, ". . .for man looketh on the outward appearance, but the Lord looketh on the heart." The prison officials evaluated me by my outward appearance, by my list of crimes, and by my age; but God saw my heart!

When I left prison, I was a nineteen year-old ex-con arrested for five felonies and countless misdemeanors. Statistics show that the odds of a person like me staying out of prison are low. . .extremely low. It was inevitable that I would someday return to prison. If anyone with my history did manage to stay out of prison, he or she would most likely lead a nonproductive life, exist on welfare, receive unemployment checks, or work menial jobs for the rest of his or her life. It would take a miracle for me to stay out of prison *and* to make something of my life.

Now, twenty four years after I was released from prison, I can honestly say that I've *lived* the miracle. My life has been completely restored. No one who encounters me today would ever recognize me as the person in this book. I'm not dragging the past around with me. Jesus has healed my life. To summarize the changes:

1. My mind has been restored. In the midst of drug abuse, there were days when I literally couldn't remember how to spell my name. Immediately after prison I returned to college. This time I consistently made straight A's. Later I attended Bible college. Every semester at Bible college, I made straight A's. Now I remember even the most minute details of life

with great clarity. This restoration is available to those who seek after Jesus. In the Bible, one insane demoniac who Jesus healed was dramatically transformed: (He was) "sitting, and clothed and in his right mind: and they were afraid" (Mark 5:15).

2. I have confidence in who I am. I'm confident in spite of my past. One day when I was praying I realized that Jesus had left heaven, come to Earth, and died for me. . .For me! That sounds so simple, but suddenly those words exploded in my heart and mind. The Scripture became personal to me. I was overwhelmed by God's love and the great value that He placed on me. In an instant the inferiority that I had felt throughout my life was washed away. In a second with God, years of pain were gone—never to return. I can courageously face people without fear. Many people spend years in counseling to get what God gave me instantaneously. Proverbs 28:1 says, "The wicked flee when no man pursueth: but the righteous are bold as a lion."

3. God placed a work ethic within me. While in college, I took a job in a printing factory. As magazines came off the press, I stacked them on a pallet. As soon as I turned around, another stack was ready to go. I did that over and over again. From the first day that I walked into the factory, I had an understanding that God could do something with me, if I would only let Him. Working in the factory was God's perfect will for me. So, I worked with passion. For two years I worked

every hour of overtime that I could. I never took a sick day. During that time, God taught me to be a reliable employee and built character in me. Today I'm forty-three years old. During my adult life, I've never taken a single penny of unemployment, welfare, food stamps, or any other government money. God taught me to work. He supplies my needs, and I don't need to rely on the government.

4. Jesus opened the door for me into the business world. One day I was praying when I clearly felt impressed to start a business. Having never had a business, I knew nothing about how to start one. I continued to pray and study. Within four months I opened a construction-related business. During the second year I wore a suit and carried a briefcase into the corporate office of Kraft, Inc. in Chicago. The head facilities engineer over every building that Kraft owns in the world met with me. I asked if my company could be approved to do his work. He approved my company. Our first job for Kraft was worth $106,850.00. When I signed the contract, I didn't even own a pickup truck. We bought one shortly thereafter. From that point on the growth has been rapid.

Today a $100,000.00 project would not be considered large for us. We've completed projects many times that size. But back then, it was a tremendous breakthrough. For seventeen years I've been founder and president of a construction-related corporation. Our business performs large commercial projects across the continental United States. Our list of clients includes Kraft, Inc., Inland Steel, RJR Nabisco, General Electric, United Technologies, Essex Corporation, Champion Laboratories, Case International Harvester, and the Wal-Mart Corporation. Not only has God provided financially for me, but He has used our efforts to provide jobs and income for many families.

5. Ministry doors have opened for me. Through the years, I have preached the Gospel of Jesus via street ministry, door to door witnessing, street drama teams, and concerts at churches, high schools, and colleges. I have shared the grace of God in jails, prisons, churches, youth groups, and anywhere God has led me. My heart's desire is to share Jesus with those who have not yet met Him.

CHAPTER

12

FATHERS

Throughout my life I often longed for a father who would love me. I wanted a father's love, discipline and strength. I wanted to be able to discuss problems with a father, to get insight and wisdom from a father. But my earthly father had no interest in filling that role.

A few months after my release from prison, I met a group of people that had formed a new church. I was asked to sing at one of their meetings. Before singing the song, I mentioned that I had written the song in prison, the place I met Jesus. When the song was over, they gave me a roaring round of applause. After the meeting, several invited me to their homes.

We became close friends. I can honestly say that I have never again longed for a father. The men who took me in that night became my new earthly fathers. They have loved me through difficult times. They have disciplined me when required. They have laughed with me and cried with me. They have blessed me with a richness beyond compare. One is the dean of a college; one is a doctor; one operates a tire shop. Some are farmers; some are teachers; some are building contractors. One is the Circuit Clerk of our county. One works for the city. Some are factory workers. One is an engineer.

I walked into their homes, fully welcomed, wondering why they would want to be with me. Day by day, God knit our hearts together. Rough times? Yes, we had plenty! Polishing a diamond requires a lot of friction, you see. Sometimes it was painful for everyone involved. I know that now, twenty four years later, not one of us involved would trade the experience. Depending upon the situation at hand, I can call upon their experience, wisdom, and knowledge. Each one at different times has been there for me as a father. For that I am eternally grateful. I Corinthians 4:15 says, "For though ye have ten thousand instructors in Christ, yet have ye not many fathers: for in Christ Jesus I have begotten you through the gospel."

Beyond these earthly fathers, I also have a heavenly Father. I have confidence that my cries reach His ears, His eyes are always on me, and His heart is tender toward me. His hand is always upon me, and His words are in my heart.

There was a time when I needed money to go to college. During an afternoon of prayer, I told God that other fathers put their children through college. I recognized that He was my Father, so I asked Him to put me through college. I needed thousands of dollars, but suddenly money began to pour in. Within *ten days,* God had supplied the entire amount. During college, I never lacked anything. In fact, while I was in college I made more money working part time than I ever had in my life. I am so glad, though, that our Father God supplies much more than money. His love for us is perfect and complete. He is our provider, healer, encourager, peace, comforter, salvation, deliverer, victory, prosperity, and health. God is a wonderful

Father. In fact, He's the perfect Father. While we were yet sinners He gave Jesus to die for our sins. After we accept Him, how much more will He be our constant and faithful companion!

During my early years, the words, "You're gonna be just like your father," were a curse spoken over me repeatedly. Until I was eighteen, that curse ran its course. After I met Jesus in prison, I began to get to know my Heavenly Father. It was after prison that the Lord blessed me with many earthly fathers who have greatly blessed my life. Now that I know my true Father, I dedicate myself to fulfilling those words that were spoken so long ago. I'm determined that, "I'm gonna be just like my Father."

EPILOGUE

I pray that every person who reads this book will see God the Father, Jesus and the Holy Spirit in a new and clearer light. May the realization that God is alive and that He cares for you be born anew in your heart. May you know that no one is beyond God's reach; no one has gone too far that he cannot be saved. May you know that God is waiting for your prayer. May you know the peace of salvation through Jesus and His shed blood. May you know the wonder of having every sin washed in the Blood of Jesus and realize His saving power. Most of all, I pray that you will know that the heart of God is kind, full of mercy and compassion. His grace is available to all who ask.

Pray with me now,

Father God, I believe that Jesus is the Son of God. I believe that He died on the cross for me. I believe that His Blood was shed for me. I believe that His Blood is the payment for my sins. Lord Jesus, I accept You as my Savior. I ask You to forgive me of my sins. I repent, Lord Jesus. I ask You to be my Lord today. Jesus, cleanse me of my sins. Heal my life. Rebuild, restore, renew, save, and free me today. Thank You, Lord Jesus—let me walk with You each day. Teach me Your ways, O Lord. Show me the way to heaven. Amen.

I pray that each of you who is a prisoner will become:
A Prisoner: **RELEASED!**

Now that you have read this book and have been confronted with the Good News of Jesus, what are you going to do with your life? If you have asked Jesus into your heart, you are on your way to heaven. But, what about the rest of the world? There is a lost and dying world out there. They need to hear about Jesus, too. Who will tell them? Won't you be the one to let your light shine? The world needs your help. Please don't spend your life on things that don't matter. In the scope of eternity, what we do with Jesus and who we share Him with are the only things that matter. Wherever you are, be bold for Jesus. Prisoner, proclaim Jesus in the prison. Student, proclaim Jesus in the school. Factory worker, proclaim Jesus in the factory. Doctor, proclaim Jesus in the hospital. Together we can increase the citizenship of heaven. After all, that is the Great Commission. Mark 16:15,16 says, ". . Go ye into all the world, and preach the gospel to every creature. He that believeth and is baptized shall be saved; but he that believeth not shall be damned."

THANK YOU

I walked out of prison twenty-four years ago with $60.00 and the clothes on my back. Today my life is completely restored. That transition did not occur in a vacuum; I did not "make it on my own." Many people helped me along the way.

One brother who got involved in my life took me down to a store and bought me my first dress clothes; a black sweater, black tie and white shirt. I remember I liked how people treated me when I wore nicer clothes. That part of my life began to change. Thanks, Larry.

To each and everyone who has given into my life, I thank you. God bless you.

A special thanks to the following:

My wife, Sherry
my best buddy Zach
Phyliss P.
Chris and Betty Boyd for feeding me, I remember.
Leslie Kent
Phyliss Bliesner
Prison Fellowship Ministries
Operation Starting Line
My entire O.S.L. Family
Tondra & Ed
Rita Lake
T. McKenney
J. & D. Simmons
Jeff Martin

K. & L. Ernst
Church of God Bible Believers- Flora
Monty Lee & Ta Kimble
D. Miller
D & B Munyon
Rick Schaff
R. & D. Schroeder
Nat and Shirley Wofford
L. Schaff
B. Rabe
D. & V. Wortman
J. Howe
L. & L. Davidson
D. Williams
L. & M. Schnautz
J. & H. Parker
P. & M. Davidson
G. & H. Birch
Christian Church of Sailor Springs
Coronado Baptist Church   El Paso
Joe and Darlene Bahr
Jan and Mike Stevens
Marvis Frazier
Melvin Adams; you too, Sammy
Phyllis Bliesner, Dorothea Jinna and Vi Wortman who encouraged me to finish this book. Thank You.
Thank you to each Prison Fellowship Ministries and Operation Starting Line teammate

Special Thanks to Billy Joe Daugherty and
Chuck Colson for endorsing A Prisoner: Released.

And, Thanks to anyone who ever feeds the hungry, clothes the naked, visits prisoners, or reaches out to a brother or a sister in Jesus' love. You are the body of Christ on this earth. Thank you.

Most importantly, I want to thank my mother, Vada, for all that she has done. Mom dedicated me to God at birth and has prayed for me each day of my life. She never gave up on me when all appeared lost, but continued in prayer. She has been able to see God answer each of those prayers. Mother, thank you for the Picture Bible and every kind thing that you have done. Thank you for living for Jesus.

Yes, Mom made mistakes, but it's all forgiven and forgotten. Jesus is a restorer and a rebuilder and He heals the past. Thank you, Jesus.

To all of the mothers who pray...Keep Praying! God answers!!!

Our Mission:

Half of America's 1,900,000 prisoners will be released this year and new prisoners will fill their beds. This turnover occurs every year. Statistics show that over eighty percent of all prisoners return to prison. Even though prisons are being built rapidly, the need for more beds still exceeds construction. Something must be done. Jesus instructed us in Matthew 25 to reach out to those who are in prison. That scripture tells me that when I look into the eyes of a prisoner, I am looking into the eyes of Jesus, my Lord and Savior. It's that simple.

Please help us do all that we can do to reach these brothers and sisters. Our mission is to place A Prisoner: Released into the hands of every prisoner in America. For every book that we sell through our ministry and for every $5.00 we receive in donations, we will donate one book to a prisoner. We have partnered with many prison ministries to distribute these free books.

Won't you help? Please consider a generous gift to help us proclaim God's restoration power. Matthew 25:40 "... Verily I say unto you, Inasmuch as ye have done it unto one of the least of these my brethren, ye have done it unto me." We can love the unlovable and reach the "unreachable."

Thank You, Brian

131

A Few Poems:

Perfect Painter

I saw an artist painting pictures
with an accomplished touch
creating life upon the canvas
with the stroke of every brush
But unlike other painters
who could only imitate
He put truth into his paintings
and they knew that He was great

So the other painters had a meeting
to plot a destiny
they said, "How can we sell our paintings
when this man paints for free?
And, the colors that He blends
are so pleasing to the eye."
the conclusion of the meeting
was this man had to die

So they turned the mob against him
and had him crucified
and the painters celebrated
the competition all had died
but before the celebration had time
to reach its end
they heard the startling news
the Artist paints again

And He painted perfect pictures
with the power to liberate
as we gazed upon His paintings
His love would overpower hate
and the owners of the paintings
would become really free
and the beauty of it all
is that He painted one for me.

Yes, the beauty of it all
He painted one for you and me.

Brian Brookheart © 1981, 1997

Father's Day

There's no one to call on Father's Day
No one to be my dad
No one to laugh when things are grand
or cry when things are sad
No one to say "hey, that a boy"
no one to say "well done"
And I've never heard my father's voice
say "I'm so proud of you son."

So Father God if you don't mind
I'll spend this day with you
And thank you for the many times
your love has brought me through
You adopted me at the greatest price
that anyone could pay
I'm so glad you're my Father God
today on Father's Day

Lord I forgive my earthly dad
I want to make that clear
and I would hug him in your love
if he was only here
Perhaps someday the phone will ring
and he'll be on the line
and his words will be a healing balm
poured on this heart of mine

Lord I know the pain I've felt
makes me who I am today,
and it's why I care for those who hurt
why I give your love away.

So Father God if you don't mind
I'll spend this day with you
And thank you for the many times
your love has brought me through
You adopted me at the greatest price
that anyone could pay
I'm so glad you're my Father God
today on Father's Day

Brian Brookheart © 2001

When Grandma Died

I did not cry when Grandma died
cause I knew where she was
For 50 years she served the Lord
and told me of his love
At evening time she'd stoke the fire
and we would sit around
She'd tell us of the Word of God
and the place where she was bound

Though I never had a dad,
I knew grandma loved me so
when Father-Son banquets came,
Grandma and I would go
though it may seem awkward,
it did not occur to me.
Grandma was my superstar,
I was as proud as I could be.

Her eyes were like the eyes of God
always looking down
Her tears taught me tenderness
when they came streaming down
Her smile would reassure me
that all would be ok
I could hear her voice in any crowd,
so I could find my way

At 88 her mind had slipped
and she did not remember me
So I asked her who Jesus was,
out of curiosity
She slipped her hands into the air
as she began to cry
Saying, Jesus is my precious Lord
and for my sins He died.

So, I did not cry when Grandma died
cause I knew where she was
For 50 years she served the Lord
and told me of his love
At evening time she'd stoke the fire
and we would sit around
She'd tell us of the Word of God
and the place where she was bound

Brian Brookheart © 2001

I'm not the best at answering my mail, but I read every letter I get. If Jesus has touched your life through this little book, we'd love to hear about it. Drop us a line at:

Brian Brookheart Ministries, Inc.
PMB # 509
44 Music Square East
Nashville, TN 37203